JOSHGIBSON

Read all of the books in this exciting, action-packed biography series!

Alex Rodriguez

Annika Sorenstam

Barry Bonds

Cal Ripken Jr.

David Beckham

Derek Jeter

Doug Flutie

Hank Aaron

Ichiro Suzuki

Jesse Owens

Jim Thorpe

Joe DiMaggio

Josh Gibson

Lance Armstrong

Michelle Kwan

Mickey Mantle

Muhammad Ali

Pelé

Peyton Manning

Roberto Clemente

Sandy Koufax

Sasha Cohen

Tiger Woods

Tim Duncan

Tom Brady

Tony Dungy

Wayne Gretzky

Willie Mays

Wilma Rudolph

Wilt Chamberlain

Yao Ming

Sports Heroes and LEGENDS™

JOSHGIBSON

by Carrie Golus

TF
CB Twenty-First Century Books/Minneapolis

Fx: 5-14

Twenty-First Century Books
A division of Lerner Publishing Group, Inc.
241 First Avenue North
Minneapolis, MN 55401 U.S.A.

Website address: www.lernerbooks.com

Front cover: © Mark Rucker/Transcendental Graphics/Getty Images.
Back cover: © Aaron Kohr/Shutterstock Images.

Library of Congress Cataloging-in-Publication Data

Golus, Carrie, 1969-
    Josh Gibson / by Carrie Golus.
        p.   cm. — (Sports heroes and legends)
    Includes bibliographical references and index.
    ISBN 978–0–7613–5367–6 (lib. bdg. : alk. paper)
    1. Gibson, Josh, 1911–1947—Juvenile literature. 2. Baseball players—United States—Biography—Juvenile literature. 3. African American baseball players—Biography—Juvenile literature. I. Title.
GV865.G53G65 2011
796.358092—dc22 [B]   2009048486

Manufactured in the United States of America
1 — VI — 7/15/10

Contents

Tall Tales

This part of the story we know is true: In 1930, nearly all baseball games were played in daylight. Stadiums, even major league stadiums, did not yet have artificial lighting.

Games featuring the Kansas City Monarchs, one of the best Negro league teams, were rare exceptions. In 1930 the Monarchs' owner bought a portable lighting system at the enormous cost of $100,000 (more than $1 million in modern money). The lights were powered by generators. They were mounted on trucks so they could travel along with the team. On July 25, the Monarchs brought their state-of-the-art system to Forbes Field in Pittsburgh, where they played a night game against the Homestead Grays.

But the lights were dim compared to modern stadium lights. Neither team—especially the Grays, who were not used to playing under artificial light—could see the ball well. The lights would dim unexpectedly from time to time. And the poles holding the lights were not very tall, so when the ball was hit high it disappeared into the night.

As the Grays' manager, William "Judy" Johnson, told the tale, pitcher Smokey Joe Williams and catcher Buck Ewing made an agreement. In these difficult conditions, Williams would throw only two kinds of pitches—a fastball and a curve ball. But Williams threw a pitch that Ewing misjudged.

The force of the ball split Ewing's finger open. He was unable to play for the rest of the game. Outfielder Vic Harris sometimes substituted for Ewing. But this time he refused to take over. He said he couldn't see well enough in the poor light to catch Williams's fast pitches.

Johnson saw eighteen-year-old Josh Gibson in the grandstand eating a hot dog. Johnson had heard about Gibson. He was a talented catcher for the Pittsburgh Crawfords, a local semiprofessional team. Players for the Crawfords and other semiprofessional teams were paid, but not very much.

Johnson sent Cumberland "Cum" Posey, the Grays' owner, to ask Gibson if he wanted to catch for the rest of the game. Gibson replied excitedly, "Yeah, oh, yeah!"

The game was stopped while Gibson changed out of his work clothes. They were filthy from the day's work in the steel mill. Gibson donned a Homestead Grays uniform and took to the field. Despite his inexperience and the bad light, Gibson was able to catch most of Williams's fast, powerful pitches. With Gibson's help, the Grays beat the Monarchs 6–5 that night. And that was how Gibson came to play in his first professional baseball game.

Although it's a great story, the tale is more entertaining than true. In fact, Gibson was not even in the ballpark for that particular Monarchs-Grays game. And the game was actually played in the afternoon. He did play his first game for the Grays the following night, July 26. But he wasn't pulled from the stands in an emergency. He just suited up with the rest of the team.

There are other stories about Gibson's introduction to baseball. Many of these stories contradict each other. For example, a *New York Daily News* sports column puts the beginning of Gibson's professional career in 1928. According to this version of events, in 1928 the Pittsburgh Crawford Juniors team was riding in a truck on the way home from a game. As the truck rounded a turn, a baseball flew over a hill and hit the truck's radiator.

When Coach Roy Sparrow climbed out of the truck to assess the damage, he spied a baseball diamond 500 feet away. Sparrow walked up to the group of young boys playing there. One of them—Gibson—looked particularly guilty.

"Did you hit that ball?" Sparrow supposedly yelled. Gibson admitted he had and asked what Sparrow was going to do to him. "What am I going to do?" the coach asked. "If you can drive a ball 500 feet I'm going to sign you up!"

Both stories are typical of the kind of folklore that grew up around Gibson and other players in what were known as the Negro leagues. The Negro leagues did not keep detailed, accurate records like the major leagues did. Without good records, fact got mixed up with fiction. With the passing decades, historians have difficulty knowing which is which.

Gibson is considered to be one of the very best players of the Negro leagues—and all of baseball. But, lacking a time machine, baseball fans will never know for sure exactly how good Gibson really was.

Chapter One

Childhood

Joshua Gibson was born on December 21, 1911, in Buena Vista, Georgia. He was the first-born child of Mark Gibson and Nancy Woodlock Gibson. Josh's younger brother, Jerry, was born in 1914. A third child, Annie, was born in 1917. Josh was named after his grandfather, who had been a slave.

Slavery was abolished by law after the Civil War (1861–1865), nearly fifty years before Josh was born. But for African Americans living in the South, little had changed since the years of legalized slavery. Black people were clearly still second-class citizens. They lived in shacks apart from where white people lived. They were subject to the Jim Crow laws, which limited where they could go and what they could do. Josh, along with his brother and sister and the other black children in Buena Vista, attended segregated schools that were not as good as the white children's schools.

Although the standard date given for Josh's birth is December 21, 1911, there is no written documentation for this. When his son, Josh Gibson Jr., requested a copy of the birth certificate, he was told that in 1911, the state of Georgia did not bother to keep records on African Americans. "Plus," he said, "they didn't send me my ten dollars back for filing the application."

Mark Gibson and other black farmers did backbreaking labor for sixty or more hours a week. But for all their hard work, their families still lived in poverty. In the rural South, there was little opportunity to get any other kind of job. For African Americans especially, the chances of improving their lives were very slim.

But life in the North was different. Newspapers owned by African Americans from the North, such as the *Chicago Defender*, the *New York Amsterdam News*, and *The Pittsburgh Courier*, spread the word among blacks in the South about a better life in northern cities.

At the time, factories in northern cities were hiring unskilled workers at good wages. Industrial centers such as Chicago, Illinois, and Pittsburgh, Pennsylvania, needed people to work in steel mills and automobile plants. Black workers earned decent money and were treated with more respect than they were in the South.

Josh's father was one of the many African Americans who decided to give it a try. In 1921 he headed north to Pittsburgh, then known as the "Smoky City" because of all the industry there. Mark traveled alone in a segregated train car. The family was to stay in Georgia until he got settled. Almost immediately, he found work in the Carnegie-Illinois Steel Company plant. The job was physically exhausting, but the money was good. The wages were much better than what he had earned in Georgia. And while Pittsburgh had its own racial problems, the city was a world away from the open contempt he had experienced as a black man in the South.

Between 1910 and 1930, more than one million African Americans moved from the South to the North. Historians have called this movement the Great Migration.

Mark Gibson worked hard and saved his money. Three years later, the family joined him. The Gibsons moved into a brick house at 2410 Strauss Street in Pleasant Valley, a mostly black neighborhood on Pittsburgh's north side. The neighborhood was also home to recent immigrants to the United States, in particular Jewish and Italian people. Years later, in one of his rare comments about his personal life, Gibson said, "The greatest gift Dad gave me was to get me out of the South."

By then, Josh was twelve years old. He started sixth grade at Allegheny Prevocational School, where he specialized in electrical studies. The next year, he enrolled in a similar program at Conroy Prevocational, a high school in Pleasant Valley.

In his free time, Josh liked to roller skate around Pleasant Valley's hilly streets. His athletic ability was obvious from a young age. He did not particularly enjoy playing football or basketball, which were popular sports in the neighborhood. But he was a fast runner—stocky with thick, strong legs—who won awards in track.

He also liked swimming and diving, and as a teenager won several medals in swim meets held at local pools. But his best sport was baseball. Josh had played the game when he lived in Georgia, but his talents really began to develop once he moved to Pennsylvania.

Josh's future looked bright, but there was trouble at home. His father suffered from high blood pressure, but he was not in a doctor's care so it was left untreated. Meanwhile, Josh's mother had begun to develop a drinking problem. Some days, neither of his parents was capable of taking care of his brother and sister, so Josh tried to help out as much as he could.

At age sixteen, after the ninth grade, Josh left school. He had the basic skills needed to enter the electrician's trade. His first job was as an apprentice electrician at Westinghouse Airbrake. The company manufactured air brakes for the railroads. Later, Josh worked in the steel mills. His bosses considered him an excellent worker. He was physically strong, even-tempered, and friendly.

Josh soon began playing on his first organized baseball team, sponsored by Gimbel's department store. The team was part of the Greater Pittsburgh Industrial League, an all-black baseball league. At the time, many Pittsburgh companies had established amateur baseball teams to provide recreation for their employees. Other teams in the league were sponsored by Garfield Steel, Homestead Steel, Pittsburgh Railways, and Pittsburgh Screw and Bolt. The games between these amateur teams often drew as many fans as those played by the Homestead Grays, the local African American professional team.

Josh's skills were so impressive that Gimbel's eventually hired him as an elevator operator just so he would keep playing on the team. Because of his size—he stood 6 feet 2 inches and weighed 200 pounds—he was put in the catcher's position on the team. But Josh found catching difficult. After being tried out in various positions, he finally settled on third base. Josh had a lot of work to do on his fielding. But his talents as a batter were obvious from the very beginning.

Chapter Two

The Negro Leagues

A modern young baseball player with Josh Gibson's kind of talent might dream of a career in the major leagues. But in the 1920s, that was not even a distant dream for Gibson. At the time, the major leagues were closed to African American players, no matter how good they were.

This limitation had not always been the case. The game of base ball—which at the time was spelled as two words—first developed as an amateur sport in the eastern United States in the early 1800s. During the Civil War, the game spread in army camps and military prisons, becoming wildly popular among both whites and blacks. The first professional league, the National Association of Professional Base Ball Players, was formed in 1871.

In the early days, most teams—amateur, professional, or semiprofessional—were segregated by race, but a few were not. Bud Fowler is said to have been the first black professional baseball player. He joined a white minor league team in New Castle, Pennsylvania, in 1872.

The first African American to play for a major league team was Moses Fleetwood Walker. Walker played for a team called the Toledo Club, which in 1884 became part of a major league, the American Association. (In the early days of baseball, leagues—even major leagues—came and went.) His brother, Weldy Wilberforce Walker, later became the second black major league player. More than sixty other African American players took part in various white leagues around this time.

❝There should be some broader cause—such as lack of ability, behavior, and intelligence—for barring a player, rather than his color.❞

—WELDY WALKER, SECOND KNOWN AFRICAN AMERICAN
PROFESSIONAL BASEBALL PLAYER

But by 1887, the winds of racism were blowing. The directors of the International League, an early league that also included Canadian teams, received complaints from white players about having to play with black players. So they stopped offering contracts to black players. The five African American players in the International League were allowed to stay. But for the first time, a professional baseball league had made it clear that the league would be whites-only.

Even as African American athletes were being shut out of the majors, they were forming all-black teams of their own. The first professional black team started out in 1885 at the Argyle Hotel, a summer resort in Babylon, New York. Called the Argyle Athletics, the team was put together by the hotel's headwaiter, who organized the other waiters into a team to entertain the hotel guests.

Later, the Argyle Athletics changed their name to the Cuban Giants and became a traveling professional team. The name was intended to suggest that they were foreigners—anything but African Americans—so they could avoid the open prejudice that African Americans faced. On the field, the players even communicated with each other in a made-up gibberish that they hoped would pass for Spanish.

As early as 1888, white sportswriters noticed that black ballplayers were excluded from the major leagues only because of skin color. They definitely did not lack talent. According to an article in *Sporting News*, "There are players among these colored men that are equal to any white players on the ball field. If you don't think so, go and see the Cuban Giants play. This club, with its strongest players on the field, would play a favorable game against such clubs as the New Yorks or Chicagos."

In 1901 the Baltimore Orioles, a major league team, decided to try to get around the color ban. John McGraw, the Orioles manager, wanted to sign Charlie Grant, a talented African American player. Grant had made a name for himself playing for an all-black team, the Columbia Giants of Chicago.

McGraw decided not to confront the ban against black players directly. Instead, he tried to pass Grant off as Native American, listing him under the name Charlie Tokohama. While Native Americans also faced discrimination, a Native American player would be more acceptable than an African American one. McGraw's plan did not fool the other owners, however. When they challenged him, McGraw dropped Grant from the team.

In the 1920s, professional black teams began to form their own leagues. Like early white leagues, however, they usually did not last long. The Negro National League was founded in 1920 and folded in 1932. A competing league, the Eastern Colored League, was founded in 1923 and collapsed in 1928. They were replaced by a new Negro National League in the Midwest and the American Negro League in the East.

The Negro leagues and the major leagues began to develop different styles of baseball. The style of play that developed among African American teams was looser and more unpredictable. Opposing teams and fans never knew what to expect, which made the games more exciting.

African American players often called their version of the game "tricky baseball." It was rougher, there were fewer rules, and the rules that existed were often bent. James "Cool Papa" Bell was a Negro leaguer who played from 1922 to 1946. Bell sometimes ran from first base to third without ever touching second. He ran about 3 feet inside second base so the distance would be shorter. Bell figured that nobody would notice. They would all be watching the ball in the outfield and not him—and he was right.

> **❝**Negro baseball was at once heroic and tawdry, a gladsome thing and a blot on America's conscience.**❞**
> —ROBERT PETERSON, IN ONLY THE BALL WAS WHITE

African American pitchers threw a number of different pitches. These included pitches that featured so-called doctored balls. Negro league pitchers had all kinds of tricks for doctoring a ball. They might coat the ball in Vaseline, hair tonic, or spit. They might cut the ball with a fingernail, a razor, or a bottle cap hidden in a back pocket. Then there was the well-known "emery ball," which had been scuffed with a rough cloth similar to sandpaper that was called an emery cloth. Doctored balls are more unpredictable and therefore much more difficult to hit. It wasn't illegal to doctor the ball in the Negro leagues, but it was controversial. (Doctoring balls is still practiced, but usually the player is caught and penalized.)

Among fans, one of the criticisms of Negro league baseball was that the players lacked technique. This did not refer to tricky baseball, but rather to the fact that black players did not always demonstrate the accepted, textbook methods of hitting, pitching, and fielding. Many African American players had just picked up the game by playing with friends and had never been taught by a coach. They had bad habits because no one had ever taught them the "proper" way to play baseball.

Gibson was an exception to this. Even though Gibson had received little formal coaching as a young man, he was a model of textbook form as a hitter. His only flaw was his stance, which was upright and somewhat stiff. But Gibson's natural strengths—his eye, his reflexes, and his overall hitting ability—more than made up for this shortcoming.

❝*It was just a treat to watch him hit the ball. There was no effort at all.*❞

—JUDY JOHNSON, GIBSON'S FIRST MANAGER

Like white teams, African American teams traveled around the country to play baseball. But black teams often had trouble finding a hotel that would rent rooms to them or restaurants that would serve them. Sometimes black teams would have to camp out on the ball field overnight if they could not find hotel rooms.

Negro league teams had to contend with racism in their own hometowns as well. In Pittsburgh, the Homestead Grays played at Forbes Field, the home of the major league Pittsburgh Pirates. The Grays paid rent to be able to use the stadium, but they were not really welcome there. The Grays and other African American teams were not allowed to use the locker rooms. Instead, black teams had to shower and dress at the local YMCA, which was across town.

Ironically, black teams often played in front of mainly white crowds. In cities where the major league team was not very impressive, such as Cincinnati in the 1930s, white fans often went to black games. But they often used ugly racist terms when talking about the black players.

Another difference between major league teams and Negro league teams was the number of games they played. To make enough money to keep the leagues going, African American teams needed to play as many games as possible during the six-month season. That meant Negro league teams often played against semiprofessional and amateur teams. Games against other league teams made up only a small part of the schedule. Sometimes, a team would play three different games in three different locations in a single day.

66We didn't have many lay-offs. Sometimes we would play three games a day—that was common. When we'd play a doubleheader, we'd think it was a holiday.99

—JUDY JOHNSON, NEGRO LEAGUE
BASEBALL PLAYER AND MANAGER

The quality of record keeping was another difference. The Negro leagues did not keep detailed, accurate records as the major leagues did. This makes it almost impossible to know all the facts about the Negro league players. For example, information about professional, semiprofessional, and amateur competitions is all lumped together. So home run totals are huge. The record shows that Gibson hit seventy-two home runs in 1933. But it is likely that most of those runs should not have been counted because they were not made in league games.

The sports pages of daily newspapers are another good source of information about early major league baseball. But the big newspapers all but ignored Negro league games. These papers were white-owned and did not bother to cover topics of interest to African Americans. The black-owned newspapers of the period, such as the *Chicago Defender*, *The Pittsburgh Courier*, *Baltimore Afro-American*, and *New York Amsterdam News*, did cover the games. But the black papers were weeklies, and sportswriters did not have the space to write about every game.

Box scores in black papers rarely included at-bats, which is the number of times a batter stepped up to the plate (with a few exceptions, such as when a player is walked). And runs batted in (RBIs) were never reported. Without this information, Negro league statistics cannot be directly compared with major league statistics. And in many cases, no written records existed at all. Negro league historians and biographers have had to rely on the memories of other players and family members for information.

White teams and African American teams did not play in the same league, but they did occasionally play each other. In the early days, salaries for professional athletes—both white and black—were a fraction of what they are in modern times. In the off-season, some white major league players formed so-called all-star teams that played exhibition games against black teams to make extra money.

These exhibition games had a particular edge to them. Negro league teams took these events very seriously. And white teams considered it a poor show to be beaten by a black team.

Nonetheless, the African American teams often won—not just because of tricky baseball, but because they were simply better.

Afterward, the white players sometimes said in public how good their black competition was. But baseball players are not reformers. No matter how many compliments they gave their Negro league counterparts, they still did not welcome them into the major leagues.

Chapter Three

Beginnings in Baseball

In 1927, when Josh Gibson first started playing for Gimbel's amateur baseball team, he could not hope to one day play on the local major league team, the Pittsburgh Pirates. If he dreamed of playing professional ball, his goal would have been the local African American team, the Homestead Grays.

The Homestead Grays formed in 1907 in Homestead, Pennsylvania, a small town a few miles from Pittsburgh. The team was first called the Murdock Grays, an integrated, though mostly black, amateur team. In the late 1920s, manager "Cum" Posey was determined to make the Grays one of the best professional teams in Pennsylvania. Posey was excellent at spotting talented players.

The Grays did not belong to an established league. They had no home field. They played all around western Pennsylvania for as many as eight months out of the year. Soon Posey was making a profit.

Pittsburgh also had a local semiprofessional team, the Crawford Giants. Originally, the team was sponsored by the Crawford bathhouse (during this time many working-class homes lacked indoor plumbing). The team was predominantly African American and included some Jewish and Italian players.

The Crawfords, commonly known as the Craws, were not as good as the Homestead Grays, but they were crowd favorites. They were even written up in the local African American weekly paper, *The Pittsburgh Courier*, from time to time. Like the Grays, the Craws played as many games as they could—as many as one hundred during the summer baseball season.

By city law, amateur and semiprofessional teams were not allowed to charge admission. Spectators were asked for a donation to watch the game. Usually, the collection was enough to cover expenses as well as a small fee for the players, who were not given a salary. Despite the Craws' semiprofessional status, the crowds were often just as large as those that came out to see the Grays.

In 1926 the Crawfords had a new owner, William Augustus "Gus" Greenlee. He hoped to turn the team into a truly professional club that could compete with the Grays. Greenlee appointed Harold Tinker, who was the team's center fielder, to be the team's new manager. (At the time, player-managers were common in baseball.) Tinker was put in charge of recruiting talented new players to try to bring the team up to a professional level.

Sometimes the Crawfords got around the law that called for voluntary contributions. During one 1930 tournament, every gate was locked except one. While admission was still technically free, everyone had to pay a "contribution" to get in. The amount of money collected using this tactic—$2,000—was much higher than usual.

Even as a teenager, Gibson was a naturally talented ballplayer just waiting to be discovered. Tinker first saw Gibson play in 1928 at an industrial league all-star game at Ammon Field, the same field where the Crawfords played. Tinker had gone to the game because two of the Crawfords played on the all-star team. Gibson was playing third base. "[H]e was very mature in his actions; you wouldn't think he was only sixteen years old," Tinker recalled later. "He played a terrific third base, and he was a power hitter even then."

Tinker knew he had to have Gibson play on the Crawfords. Immediately after the game, Tinker asked Gibson, 'Josh, how would you like to play with a real baseball team?' And he gave me that big smile of his and said, 'Yes sir.'" The next week, Gibson started with the Crawfords.

Hardworking and eager to learn, Gibson obsessively watched baseball and studied baseball players. He particularly studied other catchers, trying to understand how they threw, called pitches, and talked to the other players. Gibson also watched hitters, but hitting had always come more naturally to him. Gibson's skills were still developing, but he was not known for any significant weaknesses.

At first, Tinker put Gibson at third base. But other Crawford players, who had seen him catch on the Gimbel's team, suggested that he should play that position. So Tinker put Gibson behind the plate, displacing the previous catcher, Wyatt Turner. Turner was initially hurt that Gibson had taken over. But by the middle of the season, he was impressed with Gibson's innate talent. "If he put his bat down, I'd be ashamed to pick it up," Turner said.

Gibson soon began to develop a reputation as a power hitter. He was big and strong and preferred a heavy bat. The Crawfords had them specially made for Gibson. Gibson's bats were never used by any of the other players.

Gibson's success as a hitter, in Tinker's view, was the subtlety of his technique. "His power was in his wrists," Tinker recalled. "He had quick wrists. . . . He knew his wrists could do the job that most guys' legs and arms had to do." This meant that Gibson could wait until the ball was nearly upon him before swinging. He could hit curve balls or fastballs that other batters would simply not be able to handle.

66He [Gibson] was built like sheet metal. If you ran into him, it was like you ran into a wall.**99**

—HAROLD TINKER

Partly attracted by Gibson, the crowds at Crawford games grew. Sometimes as many as 5,000 people turned out to see the amateur team. But the Crawfords were still playing mostly for the love of the game. Even with a large crowd, the collection rarely brought in more than fifty dollars.

The situation became even worse when the Great Depression—a severe, worldwide economic slowdown—began in 1929. Black communities were hit hard and so was black baseball. Still, the Craws managed to survive. But Gibson and the other players relied on other jobs to make a living.

Meanwhile, when Gibson wasn't working or playing baseball, he was spending a lot of time with a young woman who lived near Ammon Field. Helen Mason was a pretty girl who was a year younger than Gibson. Her parents, James and Margaret Mason, had both moved up north from the South, just like Gibson's parents. Helen's father was a repairman for the city's water department. He traveled to the scene of water main leaks with a horse and buggy. The second of three daughters, Helen had been born in Pittsburgh and attended Schenley High School.

"He was so respectful that my dad thought [the world] of him," Helen's younger sister, Rebecca, recalled later. "He was nice and manly, and he seemed to want to be with our family more than his own." When Helen became pregnant, the couple decided to get married. They had a small ceremony at Macedonia Baptist Church on March 7, 1929. Both of their families, but no friends or teammates, were in attendance.

The couple could not afford the luxury of a honeymoon or a home of their own. So Josh moved into the Masons' house. He continued playing for the Crawfords and running the elevator at Gimbel's. He had no time to earn his electrician's license now that baseball had become a possibility as a profession.

By the spring of 1930, Gibson and the Crawfords were playing three times a week at Ammon Field. Their competition included some of Pennsylvania's best white semiprofessional teams. Some of these semipro teams even included major league players. At the time, professional athletes often earned extra money by playing under fake names on the days they didn't have major league games.

Gibson had improved too. That summer, he became the Craws' regular catcher. *The Courier*, which had started reporting on Craws games, mentioned him in print for the first time in 1930. He was still such an unknown, his name appeared as "Josh Gipson."

Gibson was not unknown to the Homestead Grays, however. According to Craws' manager Tinker, Gibson had not played for the Craws for long when the Grays tried to recruit him. Gibson was asked to be ready to play with the Grays at a moment's notice.

Tinker's story of Gibson's first game as a professional ballplayer is similar, but less dramatic, than Judy Johnson's. In Tinker's version, the Grays' catcher, Buck Ewing, split his finger in a twilight doubleheader. The outfielder Vic Harris temporarily stepped in as catcher. Meanwhile, Harris's brother was sent by taxi to fetch Gibson at Ammon Field, where he was playing for the Crawfords. Gibson arrived a few innings later, still wearing his Crawfords uniform. He quickly suited up as a Gray and played his first game as a pro ballplayer.

Baseball historians checked these old memories against newspapers and other sources from the time period. The truth is that Buck Ewing hurt his finger in an afternoon game against the Kansas City Monarchs, not a night game under their artificial lights. And since the Grays' backup catcher was also injured, Ewing just kept on playing.

The following night, however, Gibson did make his professional debut, playing under lights at Forbes Field. The newspapers were interested in the game because it was one of the first night games and because the two teams were intense rivals. They weren't interested in anything Gibson did—yet.

The Monarchs' portable lighting system was intended to allow working people to come to ball games. Fans also found it more pleasant to watch a game in the cool of the evening. In fact, the Negro leagues played night games five years before this happened in the major leagues.

The Monarchs-Grays game, attended by more than 10,000 fans, was exciting from beginning to end. The Monarchs were the first to score, but the Grays more than caught up in the second inning, racking up five runs. Then it was the Monarchs' turn to catch up. They tied the game at 6–6 by the seventh inning. In the ninth inning, a home run won the game for the Grays.

In his first game as a professional ballplayer, Gibson replaced Ewing as catcher in the fifth inning. He also batted in Ewing's slot, number seven in the batting order. But in his two at-bats, Gibson struck out both times. The game was not remarkable for Gibson. But while he got no hits, he made no errors either. And it was impressive that in his very first pro game he had held his own against the Monarchs, who had been Negro National League champions the year before. Gibson's talent and drive to succeed would soon make him one of the most valuable players on the Grays.

Chapter Four

Homestead Gray

Some baseball historians and fans consider the Homestead Grays team that Gibson joined in 1930 to be the best Grays team ever. In fact, some take their opinion even further, calling the 1930 Grays the all-time best team of the Negro leagues. The Grays that year not only included Gibson but two other future Hall of Famers: third baseman and manager Judy Johnson and first baseman Oscar Charleston.

Another player on the team was pitcher Smokey Joe Williams. Some historians believe that he was fifty years old at the time, but no one knew for sure. Williams was an enormous man—6 feet 6 inches tall. In 1930 he was playing his thirty-third baseball season.

Despite the remarkable level of talent on the Grays, and the fact that Gibson was still so young and inexperienced, manager Johnson played him as often as possible. After Ewing's split finger healed, he took over from Gibson as the Grays' regular catcher. Gibson was often brought into a game's later innings or at the very end of doubleheaders. Occasionally, he played in the outfield. And even in the strong Gray lineup, he batted sixth or seventh.

In his early days with the Grays, Gibson sometimes struggled to catch the pitches thrown by Williams and the other impressive Gray pitchers. Fastballs hit him in the chest and curve balls hit him in the shins. He was criticized for blocking balls rather than catching them. But Gibson was praised from the beginning for his accurate throwing. This is a critical skill for catchers, who are expected to throw out runners when they try to steal bases.

Gibson knew he had a lot to learn, and he chose Judy Johnson for his mentor. At the beginning of his career, Gibson lacked confidence in his catching. After every game, Gibson would ask Johnson what he had done wrong and what he could do better.

Gibson liked to give his teammates nicknames. Although his mentor Johnson was already nicknamed "Judy," Gibson called him "Jing."

To his teammates, Gibson seemed to think about baseball every minute of every day. He also put in extra time—catching batting practice before games, for example—to sharpen his defensive skills.

On August 7, two weeks after Gibson joined the Grays, the team traveled to Kansas City to play another series against the Monarchs. That day Smokey Joe Williams struck out twenty-seven players, which is a record in the Negro leagues. Since there are twenty-seven outs in a nine-inning game, that means every single out in the game came from Williams striking a batter out.

Cum Posey, the Grays' owner, wanted others to think highly of his ball club. He banned card games in the clubhouse and required the players to wear suits and ties when they came to the park.

The Monarchs' pitcher was nearly as impressive. Even though his team lost, he managed to strike out nineteen batters. With performances like that from his teammates and opponents, eighteen-year-old Gibson barely made a mark during the early part of his rookie season.

Still, for Gibson, everything seemed to be falling into place. He had achieved his dream of becoming a professional baseball player, and Helen was about to have twins. But just weeks after he joined the Grays, he suffered a profound personal tragedy.

On August 11, Gibson's sister-in-law phoned the ballpark clubhouse pleading to speak to him. Helen, who was eight months pregnant, had gone into premature labor. Her pregnancy had aggravated an unknown kidney condition. By the time Helen reached the hospital, one of her kidneys had ruptured. She lapsed into a coma. Just a few hours later she died.

The doctors at the hospital were able to save the babies, a boy and a girl. But Gibson was completely overwhelmed by the loss of his wife and the responsibility of having twin babies. He was not able to take care of them himself.

Gibson said that he did not want the children to live with his parents. With his mother suffering from alcoholism, the Gibson home would not have been a stable environment for the children. Other than making that decision, Gibson withdrew completely. He did not even name the babies. Eventually they were christened Josh Gibson Jr. and Helen, after their parents. Josh Jr. later said he was not sure if his father or if his maternal grandparents had named them.

❝He never talked to me about my mother. All I knew was, my mother died, period. That's all I knew.❞

—JOSH GIBSON JR.

Gibson also distanced himself from his late wife's family. He moved back in with his own parents, brother, and sister. Josh Jr. and Helen were raised by Helen's mother and her sisters. Gibson returned to the Grays without telling a single man on the team what had happened. Traveling with the team, Gibson rarely saw his children. Perhaps because he was so young, he was unable to be a proper father to the twins. And as his fame increased, his relationship with them became even more distant.

Even more single-mindedly than before, Gibson threw himself into learning everything he could about baseball. He rarely wrote letters home. According to his teammates, he did not enjoy reading or any other interests. Gibson's life was centered on baseball and nothing else. Because of his determination and focus, as well as his natural talents, Gibson developed very quickly as a baseball player. He had already come to the attention of the African American press by the fall of his rookie season.

In September, the Grays were finishing up a ten-game championship series against the Lincoln Giants. The series began with a doubleheader at Forbes Field in Pittsburgh. In the second game, Gibson hit a triple—and a 460-foot home run.

Afterward, *The Pittsburgh Courier* ran a photo of Gibson on the front page of the sports section. The caption identified Gibson as the Grays' nineteen-year-old catcher, "whose terrific hitting and fine receiving was one of the sensations of the opening colored world series battles at Forbes Field Saturday." In his weekly column, W. Rollo Wilson, the *Courier*'s sportswriter, gave Gibson his first nickname. He called him "Samson," after the biblical strongman.

The following week, as the series continued, Wilson devoted most of his column to Gibson. "He's green but the ripening process is moving apace," Wilson wrote. "He has not mastered the technique in throwing to second base but he kills off all the fast boys who try to steal."

Wilson's write up included the first published account of Gibson's legendary professional debut: that he had been yanked out of the grandstand to play. Most of the column added to the mythology about Gibson, such as his enormous appetite. "He spends more money for 'snacks' than any of the other players lavish on three meals," Wilson wrote. He also claimed that Gibson liked to unnerve the batters on the other team by teasing them. "They should have named him Josher instead of Joshua, for he sure can kid with the kidders."

The very day that Wilson's column appeared, Gibson added more material to his legend. The final games in the Grays-Giants series were scheduled for New York's Yankee Stadium, a first for Negro league baseball. The Giants' pitcher was Cornelius "Connie" Rector, one of the best pitchers of the era. Gibson hit two home runs off him, which were the fourth and fifth homers hit by all players in the series. The second of these two homers made its way into baseball mythology.

The *New York Amsterdam News*, New York's black weekly paper, reported that Gibson hit a 460-foot home run into the left-field bleachers. *The Pittsburgh Courier* wrote that it was "a distance of over four hundred thirty feet, with two on the bases, in the first inning."

But Judy Johnson—the same dubious source of Gibson's professional debut story—claimed that the hit had cleared the roof of Yankee Stadium and was never seen again. If this were true, Gibson would be the only baseball player to ever hit a fair ball out of Yankee Stadium. Yankee Stadium was enormous, with high outfield bleachers far from home plate. No one—not even the great home run hitter Babe Ruth, who played home games there with the New York Yankees for fourteen years— ever managed to achieve that. Another group of witnesses claimed the ball did not go into the bleachers but came down behind the left-field fence. Baseball historians have calculated that such a trajectory would have made it a 500-foot hit.

In an interview eight years after the fact, Gibson spoke simply about his infamous home run. "I hit the ball on a line into the bull pen in deep left field," he said in 1938. In later versions of the myth, the length of his Yankee Stadium hit grew to as long as 600 feet. When asked about the homer, Gibson would just smile. If that's what fans wanted to believe, that was fine with him.

Baseball historians have pointed out that Gibson seemed to respond well to particularly challenging conditions. He performed well in Yankee Stadium, which had very high walls. And he often hit best against the best pitchers.

In the fall, the Homestead Grays began a new tradition that would continue for many years. Exhibition games against white teams were held across the country. The white teams were billed as all-star teams, and the players were drawn from the major leagues. But usually they included just one big star, such as pitcher Jerome "Dizzy" Dean of the St. Louis Cardinals. The rest of the players were just run-of-the-mill major leaguers. Dean in particular was a regular on these teams. He liked the looser style of ball played in the Negro leagues and enjoyed playing black teams during the off-season.

According to some reports, Gibson ended his rookie season with a batting average of .367 with 6 homers in 32 games against professional black teams. But when the season ended, ordinary life resumed. Gibson went back to his regular jobs, working as an elevator operator at Gimbel's and the late shift in the steel mill. This life was a lot less glamorous than hitting home runs in Yankee Stadium. But as the Depression worsened, Gibson was grateful to have the work.

The Great Depression hurt baseball just like everything else. Despite top performances by black players, 1931 was a hard year financially for all Negro league teams. It was also a tough year for major league teams, which asked their players to take salary cuts.

In the spring of 1931, Gibson went to Hot Springs, Arkansas, to prepare for his first full season with the Homestead Grays.

Though it was only his second year with the team, nineteen-year-old Gibson was already an up-and-coming star. The crowd recognized him when he stepped up to bat and was excited to see what he would do. Like the previous year, he batted sixth or sometimes seventh in the lineup.

According to some baseball historians, in 1931 the Grays were possibly even better than they had been in 1930. Gibson routinely hit doubles, triples, and home runs. The Negro league did not keep official records during Gibson's first full summer playing with the Grays. But against all levels of competition—amateur, semipro, and professional teams—Gibson is credited with seventy-five home runs that year.

Judging this record is difficult, however. No official statistics are available on how many games the Grays played or how many of the games were played against top-ranked competitors. Many baseball historians have suggested that the figure is too high. On the other hand, at least one biographer has hinted it may be too low. Since many of the ballparks that Negro league teams played on did not have fences, outfielders would simply stand 400 feet away when Gibson came up to the plate, then wait for one of his long drives so they could catch it. In a major league ballpark, which would typically have a wall or fence, these long hits would have been home runs.

People came to expect Gibson's powerful hits, so these feats were barely even mentioned in news coverage of Grays games. *The Pittsburgh Courier* usually mentioned that Gibson's hitting had been the highlight of the game. But because his strong hitting happened with such regularity, it was almost not newsworthy. By the end of the 1931 season, Gibson had established himself as the cleanup hitter and the star of the Grays' lineup.

Chapter Five

The Black Babe Ruth: Facts and Legends

Gibson's impressive hitting was the result of his quick wrists, according to Craws manager Harold Tinker. But other observers claimed that his power came from his terrifically strong arms, shoulders, and back. Most contemporary observers agree that Gibson's hits were made with little apparent effort. And despite his size, Gibson was a fast runner.

When he stepped up to the plate, he stood with his feet spread wide apart. He held his heavy bat at the end, high above his right shoulder. Gibson was endlessly compared to Babe Ruth, but his batting style was quite different. Ruth, Mickey Mantle, and other power hitters of the major leagues each took a long stride—a foot or a foot and a half—as they swung at the ball. They threw their entire body into the pitch. With such a technique, a hitter connected with the ball with tremendous force. But if he missed, he was completely, even comically off-balance.

Gibson's style was just as effective but nowhere near as dramatic. Some contemporary observers say Gibson strode only slightly toward the pitch, about 4 inches. Others claim he did not stride at all, just set his foot down in the exact same spot when the pitch arrived. He also had a noticeably short swing. The final result was just as powerful as Ruth's but without the showmanship.

In fact, Gibson patterned his batting style after Ruth's sometime teammate, Lou Gehrig of the Yankees. If Gibson happened to be in a city where the Yankees were playing, he made every effort to see the game so he could watch Gehrig.

Gibson also admired Jimmie Foxx of the Philadelphia Athletics. After Ruth retired, Foxx became a top hitter in the major leagues. Foxx wore the sleeves of his uniform rolled up, both for style and to show off his powerful arm muscles. Almost from the beginning of his professional baseball career, Gibson did the same.

Gibson also had the quality of courage, an important trait in a hitter. People have a natural tendency to step away from something that is thrown at them, especially if the thing is traveling at up to 90 miles per hour. When Gibson became a top hitter, pitchers deliberately threw the ball at him. In a pinch, many Negro league pitchers used the so-called beanball, a ball thrown directly at a batter's head (bean was a slang term for head). Throwing a beanball was not considered cheating (and is still not in the major leagues). It was simply a strategic weapon used against hitters who were as good as Gibson.

Gibson's home runs were usually long drives—sometimes high, but not always. And unlike some home run hitters who were fairly predictable, outfielders never knew where the balls would end up: center, left, or right field.

66A homer a day will boost my pay.**99**

—JOSH GIBSON

Gibson was always an "average" hitter during his career, meaning he hit for a high average, not just home runs. He rarely struck out and was not fooled by balls that had been doctored, as they so often were in the Negro leagues.

Many of his opponents claimed that no other player hit balls as powerfully as Gibson did. A number of legends built on this reputation. In one game in York, Pennsylvania, Gibson reportedly hit a single so hard that when the shortstop caught the ball, the force split his skin right through the glove.

According to another Gibson tale, he was playing at Comiskey Field in Chicago. At this major league stadium, the center-field wall was 435 feet from home plate. The loudspeakers were mounted to the wall about 8 feet off the ground. Gibson supposedly hit a drive that stayed low and smashed into the loudspeaker so hard that it stuck there. The game had to be stopped while a groundskeeper pried the ball free. (Of course, the players could have just used another ball, but that would not make such a good story.)

In Washington D.C.'s Griffith Stadium, which was surrounded by 20-foot-high fences covered with billboards, Gibson hit a line drive that slammed into the fence behind right field. The ball hit an ad for hot dogs, knocking paint and dust everywhere. A quick-witted fan shouted out, "Josh knocked the mustard off that dog!"

Another undated, unsubstantiated legend is set in Forbes Field in the 1930s. Supposedly, Gibson hit the ball so high and far that no one saw it hit the ground. The umpire waited a few minutes. When the ball didn't come back into sight, he declared it a home run. The next day, the Crawfords were playing a game in Philadelphia, 300 miles away. Suddenly, from out of nowhere, a ball dropped out of the sky and was caught by the startled center fielder of the opposing team. As the story goes, the umpire pointed at Gibson and yelled, "You're out, yesterday in Pittsburgh!"

Of course, legends abound about power hitter Babe Ruth. But in Ruth's case, a written record helps to sort out fact from fiction. With Gibson, no such record exists.

According to the stories, Gibson sometimes hit more than one home run in a game, especially when playing against non-league teams. Against one semipro team in Zanesville, Ohio, he hit four homers in four at-bats. In Fairmont, West Virginia, he hit three in a row. Anecdotes like these, which have no written documentation to back them up, are what contribute to the claims that Gibson hit more than a thousand home runs in his career. Unfortunately, such statistics are impossible to verify.

Teammates have said that Gibson rarely worried when he was at bat, even if he had already racked up two strikes and it was an important moment in the game. He didn't change his stance or his grip on the bat. He seemingly remained entirely confident that he would be able to hit the ball.

According to another story told by teammate Jack Marshall, Gibson once caught himself mid-mistake. In a game against the American Giants in Indianapolis, Indiana, pitcher Sonny Cornelius threw a slow curve ball. Gibson began his swing, then realized a different kind of pitch was coming. He had already let go of the bat with his left hand, so he hit the ball with only his right, as if he were swatting at a fly. Nonetheless, Gibson managed to hit it 375 feet and over the wall.

Larry Brown, an excellent catcher in the Negro leagues, had the job of helping pitchers figure out how to defeat Gibson. Brown said that in all the games he played against Gibson, he could not figure out his weakness. Many times, after a pitcher had struck Gibson out and figured that he could do it again, "Josh came back and knocked the pitch out of the park," Brown said.

The one pitcher who did give Gibson a hard time—as well as every other hitter in the Negro leagues—was Satchel Paige. Gibson's hits against Paige were "few and far between," Gibson said. He never hit effortless homers when Paige was pitching. But Paige also said that Gibson was tough to go up against and that it was almost impossible to figure out Gibson's weakness. Paige claimed he had seen Gibson hit a ball off the scoreboard in Chicago's Wrigley Field—a distance of 700 feet.

Catching did not come naturally to Gibson the way that hitting did. Catching can be a difficult, painful job. Catchers spend most of the game in a squat, which is tough on the knees. They have to tolerate foul balls, wild pitches, swinging bats, and even the occasional base runner crashing into them at full running speed. At the same time, a catcher needs to keep his head, calling the pitches and throwing out any base runners who try to steal. Good catchers are often not good hitters.

LeRoy "Satchel" Paige was a legendary pitcher in the Negro leagues and later in the major leagues. Paige, who was born around 1905, was raised in poverty in Mobile, Alabama. He got his nickname from carrying—or, in one version of the story, from stealing—the satchels (bags) of travelers at the local train station.

Paige started in the Negro leagues by pitching for the Chattanooga Black Lookouts in 1926. In his long career, he played for the Crawfords (1932–37), the Kansas City Monarchs (1939–47), the Philadelphia Stars (1946–50), the Cleveland Indians (1948–49), and the St. Louis Browns (1951–53).

Paige was a showman as well as an athlete. He sometimes wound up two or three times before delivering the pitch. Another running joke was to have all the other members of the team leave the field except for the catcher, so Paige faced off against the batter completely on his own. He had comical names for many of his specialized pitches, including the Hesitation Pitch, the Four-Day Creeper, the Nothin' Ball, the Trouble Ball, the Two-Hump Blooper, the Midnight Creeper, and the Aspirin.

Paige's theatrical style contrasted strongly with Gibson's. Gibson was pure baseball, with little if any show. The two men had a strong rivalry and a great deal of respect for each other's talents.

Gibson was sometimes criticized for his catching. Foul balls were a particular weakness. Gibson sometimes got dizzy as he looked up to try to catch the ball. Whoever was playing first base would sometimes help out by catching these balls for him.

But Gibson did have a strong and accurate throwing arm. Speed is the most important factor in attempting to throw out base stealers. When Gibson saw someone trying to steal, he threw the ball from behind his ear while he was still in a crouching position. This was textbook catcher's form, which Gibson had worked hard to get absolutely right.

 With his powerful throwing arm, Gibson won the long-distance toss in an informal track meet among the Crawfords before a 1932 game.

One of Gibson's assets as a catcher was that he did not get hurt very often. The only recurring problem Gibson had was a shoulder that would pop out of joint, a condition that had bothered him since childhood. Whenever this happened, one of Gibson's teammates would run over and help him jerk it back into place. After a few practice throws, Gibson was ready to play again as if nothing had happened.

Gibson loved to eat vanilla ice cream, which he would devour by the quart.

Gibson's catching remained controversial throughout his career. Some teammates and sportswriters said he was a natural. Others said that his catching was a definite weakness but that it developed over time. "I can remember when he couldn't catch this building if you threw it at him," recalled outfielder Jimmie Crutchfield, who played with Gibson on the Crawfords from 1932 to 1936. "He was only behind the plate because of his hitting. And I watched him develop into a very good defensive catcher. He was never given enough credit for his ability as a catcher. They couldn't deny that he was a great hitter, but they could deny that he was a great catcher. But I know!"

Chapter Six

Pittsburgh Craws

During 1931, while Gibson was becoming a star on the Homestead Grays, his first team was undergoing major changes. The Pittsburgh Crawfords had been taken over by William A. "Gus" Greenlee, an African American entrepreneur with various business interests. Some of his interests were legal, some less so. Greenlee was determined to turn the Craws into a professional team to rival the Grays. Greenlee made this clear almost immediately, when he signed Satchel Paige.

The Craws usually played at Ammon Field and occasionally at Forbes Field. But Greenlee wanted his team to have its own stadium, so he paid for the construction of Greenlee Field. The stadium seated only 6,000 spectators, but in all other respects it was proportioned like a major league ballpark. There was even a permanent lighting system.

GUS GREENLEE

Gus Greenlee was one of the most influential businessmen in the history of the Negro leagues. He made most of his money as a racketeer and nightclub owner. He helped the people in Pittsburgh's black community in the 1930s by giving business advice and lending money. Greenlee bought the Crawfords in 1930. He then built Greenlee Field, which was used by black college football teams and by the Pittsburgh Pirates (the National Football League team that eventually became the Steelers).

Next, Greenlee needed to build up his team. To Posey's dismay, Greenlee started by poaching some of the best players from the Homestead Grays. He signed Oscar Charleston as manager, Judy Johnson as third baseman, and Ted Page as outfielder. Then he decided to go after Gibson.

In early February 1932, Posey offered Gibson his usual contract renewal for the Grays. Gibson signed the contract, which offered him $150 a month, a $25 increase from the previous year. The very next day, Greenlee phoned Gibson and offered $250 a month if he played for the Crawfords. Not only was the money better, but the chance to play with the Crawfords meant a new ball field and an exciting new team with ambitions to be the best in the Negro leagues. Gibson was attracted by the fact that the tough, competent Charleston would be managing the team, while his mentor, Johnson, was on third base. So Gibson signed the Crawfords contract too.

Posey was furious when he found out. He used his weekly column in *The Pittsburgh Courier* to try to shame Gibson into honoring the original contract. In the column, Posey wrote that Gibson had been "induced" to sign with the Crawfords. "As Gibson is very young, he is easily advised," Posey wrote, claiming that Gibson had been "poorly advised."

But in the Negro leagues, all the players were free agents. The contracts they signed were more binding on the owner than on the player. Also, there was no clause that bound players to their team unless they were traded, as was usual in the major leagues. Gibson was certainly not the first player to break a contract or sign more than one.

Posey made threats in his column, writing that Gibson "will not play in Pittsburgh. Today, baseball is a business. It is time an example was made of a few players who have no respect for their signed obligations but will jump to any club for a few dollars more." But these were empty threats that Posey could not back up. As much as some owners wished otherwise, the prospect of being locked out of the Negro leagues was very unlikely.

Gibson never explained publicly why he signed both contracts. Either he didn't understand what he was doing or he had done it deliberately. In the end, he decided to honor the second contract, with the Crawfords. In February, Gibson boarded a bus headed for Hot Springs, Arkansas, for spring training—riding a brand-new team bus that cost $10,000. It was a big change from the way Gibson had traveled with the Grays, crammed into two cars with their luggage piled on the back.

Conditions for the Crawfords were excellent compared to other Negro league teams. They had good uniforms and equipment, including two bats per player. Players on some other Negro teams had to bring their own bats.

On the way to spring training, Gibson suddenly had an appendicitis attack. He was taken off the bus and rushed to a small hospital, where his burst appendix was removed. In a hospital, this was a routine operation, but if the episode had occurred while Gibson was in a more isolated rural area, the results could have been fatal.

Gibson spent two weeks in bed before he was finally allowed to walk around. By mid-March, he still had not recovered enough to play and posed for the Craws' team picture in his street clothing. When the team returned to Pittsburgh in mid-April, Gibson was put in left field until he had completely recuperated. His hitting was still impressive, though, and he remained a successful base stealer.

In 1932 the Craws were not members of any league, because Greenlee preferred it that way. He figured the team could make more money if it played every game it was offered. Between March 25 and July 21, the Craws played 94 games in 109 days. They would have played thirteen more, but those games were rained out.

The games included the April opening of Greenlee Field, when the Craws took on the New York Black Yankees. It was an exciting game—for eight innings, every single batter on both teams struck out. The Yankees finally scored a run in the ninth. Gibson also finally connected with the ball in the ninth inning, but his hit was caught just inside the wall. The Craws lost 1–0.

In early May, the Craws took on their hometown opponents, the Grays, in a five-game series. The series would grow into a popular tradition that was hyped in the *Courier* for weeks. The 1932 Grays were still a strong team, even though they had lost Gibson and several other top players to the Crawfords. The Craws eventually won three games out of five but had to fight hard to do it.

In September, Gibson hit another one of his legend-ary home runs, in a game against the Black Yankees in York, Pennsylvania. The stadium was located next to the Pennsylvania Turnpike. The newspaper record of Gibson's hit noted that "Gibson, Crawfords catcher, tied the score in the fourth with a home run that cleared the left field fence and the pike." But in Cool Papa Bell's version of the tale, the ball flew out of the ballpark onto the back of a long-distance truck, which kept driv-ing until it reached its destination. How Bell knew exactly what became of the truck is unclear, but he claimed that Gibson had hit a 500-*mile* home run.

Later that month, the Crawfords met the Grays for another series, and this time, the Craws lost. Still, Gibson and the Crawfords won every series in 1932 except for two. The other loss came in May against the Black Yankees. At the end of the season, the Crawfords had compiled an unofficial record of 99 wins, 36 losses and were regarded as the best team in Negro league baseball.

The 1932 Pittsburgh Crawfords included five future members of the Baseball Hall of Fame: Josh Gibson, Satchel Paige, Cool Papa Bell, Oscar Charleston, and Judy Johnson.

Greenlee released Gibson's statistics at the end of the season. He claimed that in 123 games, against all levels of competition, Gibson had a .380 average and had hit 34 homers in 190 at-bats. Baseball historians have gone back and tried to correct the record by looking at box scores and game reports for games against professional competition only. Their stats are more modest but still show solid numbers: Gibson hit 7 home runs and 5 triples and had a .286 average in 46 games and 147 at-bats.

In October of 1932, Gibson traveled south to Puerto Rico to play winter ball for the Santurce Cangrejeros. Typical of his attitude toward his children, Gibson did not mention the trip to Margaret Mason, his wife's sister, until the day before he left. He promised to send them more money from the extra he earned playing winter ball. He did not keep his promise. Mason and his children heard nothing from Gibson during the three months he was away.

In his first season with the Cangrejeros, he was paid $250 a month. He was a star from the very beginning, idolized by his Puerto Rican fans. According to one story, at San Juan's Escambron Stadium, the outfield wall was surrounded by a ring of trees about 50 feet away. Gibson's frequent home runs often disappeared into the trees. After each one, the groundsmen at the stadium hung a permanent marker at the point where the fly ball had last been seen. After Gibson had been playing at the stadium for a while, the trees were so covered with markers they looked as if they were decorated for Christmas.

The amazing stories about Gibson continued when he was playing winter ball. According to one tale, Gibson was playing ball in a Puerto Rican stadium located next to a prison. As the story goes, Gibson hit a home run over the ballpark fence and over the prison fence, nearly injuring inmates who were in the prison yard—525 feet from home plate.

❝I've found freedom and democracy here, something I never found in the United States. I was branded a Negro in the United States and had to act accordingly. Everything I did, including playing ball, was regulated by my color. Well, here in Mexico I am a man.**❞**

—SHORTSTOP WILLIE WELLS, AFTER SIGNING UP
TO PLAY WITH VERA CRUZ IN THE MEXICAN LEAGUES

In 1933 Greenlee decided the Crawfords would join the Negro National League. The league included the Grays, the Detroit Stars, the Indianapolis ABCs, the Columbus Bluebirds, and the Chicago American Giants.

WINTER BALL

In the 1930s, many U.S. baseball players, both black and white, spent the off-season playing *beisbol* in Puerto Rico, Mexico, and other Latin American countries. Outdoor sports could be played all year in these warmer climates.

At the time, salaries for U.S. baseball players were a fraction of what they are in modern times. Many ballplayers jumped at the chance to earn extra money, and the salaries in Latin America were often much higher—sometimes two or three times what they were in the United States.

U.S. baseball was struggling during the Depression, so some players stayed in Latin America through the regular summer season. The higher salaries were one attraction, but for African American players the lack of racial prejudice was equally important. In Latin America, there was no color line. White, black, and Latino athletes all played together in front of Latin American crowds. And regardless of race, talented players were idolized and treated as celebrities.

Even the language barrier did not present a problem. "When you get hungry enough," Gibson once said, "you find yourself speaking Spanish pretty well." Gibson, like many of the African American players, was tempted by the money and adulation he received in Latin American countries. But he never settled outside the United States permanently.

Josh played catcher for most of his career.

Josh *(top row, fourth from right)* played for the Homestead Grays in 1931.

Josh *(far right)* poses with Satchel Paige *(second from right)* and other players in front of the Pittsburgh Crawfords team bus in the mid-1930s.

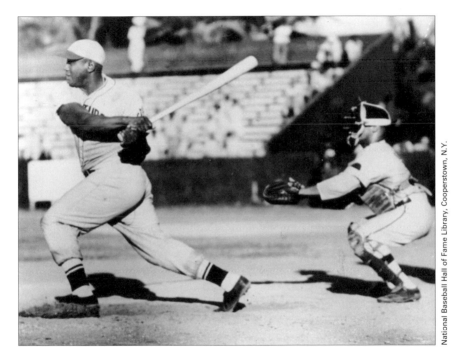

Josh at bat in a 1941 game in Sixto Escobar Park in San Juan, Puerto Rico.

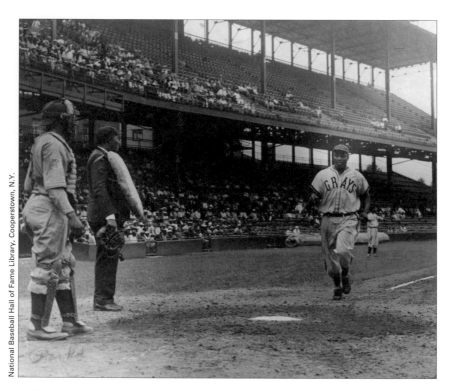

Josh completing a home run in a Homestead Grays game in 1942.

Josh rounds the bases during a 1943 Homestead Grays game.

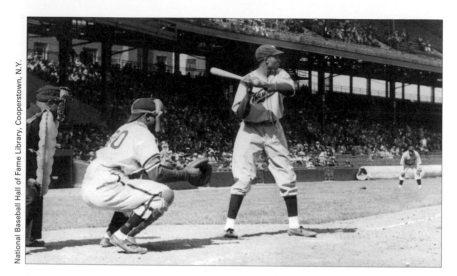

Josh behind the plate during a game in the 1940s.

Josh slides safely into home during the 1944 East-West Negro League All-Star Game at Comiskey Park in Chicago.

Josh talks to fans.

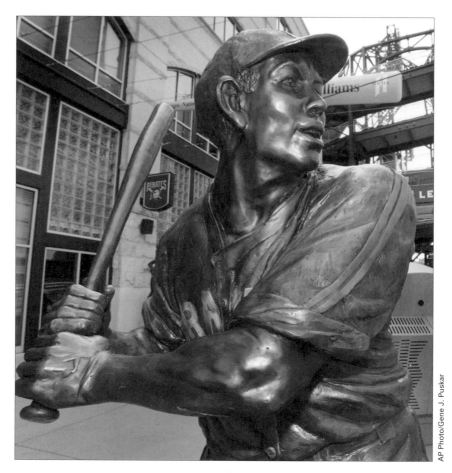

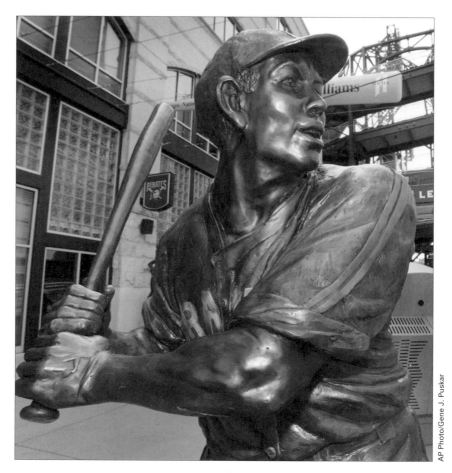

This statue of Josh was unveiled in Legacy Square in Pittsburgh, Pennsylvania, before the 2006 Major League Baseball All-Star Game.

AP Photo/Gene J. Puskar

According to Greenlee's record keeping, Gibson had 55 home runs and a .467 average in 1932. This was nearly 100 points higher than the second-best Crawford hitter, Oscar Charleston. The actual figures don't mean much because the competition was so varied. But they do show how Gibson compared with his teammates at a time when the Crawfords were one of the best teams in African American baseball.

Contemporary research holds that against professional competition, Gibson hit .362 with 6 home runs in 34 games and 116 at-bats in 1933. Then there was Cool Papa Bell's version. Years later, he swore that he had kept a record of all of Gibson's home runs and that the total that year was sixty-eight.

The first Negro leagues all-star game was played in 1933 at Chicago's Comiskey Park. Later known as the East-West game, this was an all-black version of the major league all-star game. The white all-star game, which included a home run by Babe Ruth, was part of the city's World's Fair celebration. In the Negro leagues all-star game, the players were chosen by black fans, who voted on a mail-in ballot included in black newspapers.

For Gibson, who played on the "East" team, the all-star game was an uncharacteristically weak performance. He got no home runs and just one base hit. Even worse, when he was behind the plate he made a poor throw. He tried to pick off

Sammy Bankhead when he was trying to steal second. But the wild throw went into foul territory behind right field. Bankhead not only made it to second but he ran all the way home. The West won the game 11–7.

Also in 1933, Gibson met Hattie Jones, who worked as a housekeeper in Pittsburgh. The following spring the couple began living together in a common-law marriage arrangement. Gibson bought a two-story brick town house for $1,000 at 2157 Webster Avenue on Pittsburgh's north side, not far from the house where his parents lived.

In 1934 a combined squad of Crawfords and Philadelphia Stars played several games against an all-star white team headed by Dizzy Dean. Dean, pitcher for the St. Louis Cardinals, had just finished a 30-win season ending with a World Series victory.

In one game against Dean's team, in York, Pennsylvania, Gibson hit a home run over the center-field wall in his first turn at bat. In his second at-bat, he hit the ball again over the center-field wall—this one even longer. Dean threw his hands in the air and theatrically walked away from the pitcher's mound as Gibson ran the bases. Dean played in right field for the rest of the game, an 11–1 win by the African American team. Dean reportedly told Gibson afterward that if he and Paige were on the Cardinals, "We'd win the pennant by July Fourth and go fishing the rest of the season."

Gibson was known for rarely losing his temper on the field. During one of the games against Dean's team came a rare exception. Another player's argument with the umpire had escalated into a bench-clearing fight. Gibson had been dragged into it and was fighting with catcher George Susce. Fearful for Susce's safety, Dean and Ted Page grabbed Gibson's shoulders and tried to pull him off.

Gibson reached back, picked Dean up under the armpit with one hand, and threw him across the field. As the story goes, Dean landed on his back 10 feet away. Dean burst out laughing at being thrown so far. The sight of Dean flat on his back and laughing about it calmed down the situation, and amazingly the game continued without incident. Afterward, Gibson "was kind of scratched up and had lost his cap in the scuffle, but he had a big grin on his face, you know, one of those satisfied grins, like, 'Well, that was a good one,'" Ted Page recalled years later.

During a 1934 game against the Chicago American Giants, Jack Marshall, an infielder for the Giants, claimed that Gibson hit one out of Yankee Stadium. According to Marshall, the megahit happened in the second game of a four-team double-header. Supposedly, Gibson got the hit off pitcher Slim Jones. The ball traveled to left center and over the triple deck. "They say a ball has never been hit out of Yankee Stadium," Marshall said. "Well, that is a lie! Josh hit the ball over that triple deck next to the bullpen in left field. Over and out!" Baseball historian and author Robert Peterson reported the story as truth. "A strong case can be made for the proposition that Josh Gibson, a right-hand batter, had more power than the great Babe," Peterson wrote.

Of course, no contemporary written record exists to back up Marshall's story, and Gibson himself never made such a claim. Nearly a decade later, when Gibson was summarizing his career highlights for the *Courier*, he mentioned a 1930 home run against the Lincoln Giants. He also mentioned a hit in Monessen, Pennsylvania, claiming it was the longest of his career. (The mayor of Monessen famously stopped the game so the distance could be measured.) But he did not mention an out-of-the-park homer in Yankee Stadium.

Nonetheless, Gibson's myth continued to grow. In 1935 an article in *The Pittsburgh Courier* described him as the black Babe Ruth—the first time that this nickname appeared in print. It was an important milestone not only in Gibson's career but in the myth-making that would happen around him. According to the article, Gibson had hit 72 home runs in 1933, 69 in 1934, and was out to set a new record in 1935.

The *Courier*'s home run totals did not separate league games from semipro competition, however. Years later, baseball historians reconstructed Gibson's 1934 statistics and came up with a very different figure. Against league teams that year, Gibson hit 12 home runs (a league high) in 190 at-bats, for a .295 average. Gibson was still an impressive hitter, but he wasn't a superhero.

Chapter Seven

Empty Promises

In 1936, when Gibson was in Puerto Rico, Greenlee sent him the usual contract renewal. Gibson asked for $300 a month, which would bring him up to the salary that Satchel Paige earned. But money was tight, and thinking that Gibson would give in, Greenlee refused.

Unexpectedly, Gibson decided to hold out. By now he was twenty-five years old, and he was starting to realize what a valuable player he was. Just as important, he had received a few other offers. The Philadelphia Stars had offered Gibson a deal as a player-manager at a higher salary. His old team, the Homestead Grays, was another possibility.

At the end of the 1936 season, Gibson had played a few games for the Grays during a lull in the Crawfords' schedule. Now the Grays' owner, Cum Posey, wanted him back on the team for good.

Rather than signing him out from under Greenlee, however, Posey offered to trade for Gibson for the huge sum of $2,500. According to the deal, Gibson and his mentor, third baseman Judy Johnson, would come to the Grays in exchange for the Grays' catcher and third baseman. In the African American press, this was quickly named the "Punch and Judy" trade, with the "Punch" referring to Gibson's ability as a power hitter. In March, the cash-and-trade deal went through. Gibson was once again a Homestead Gray.

In April Gibson reported to the Grays' training camp in Jacksonville, Florida. Immediately, his presence transformed the team. They would often score ten or more runs per game. "He made the whole team better, more confident," recalled first baseman Buck Leonard. "He put life into us. We felt like major leaguers then." An April game against the Miami Clowns, a 10–7 victory for the Grays, was typical. Gibson hit two home runs and a double. In the *Courier*, the headline above the box score was "Too Much Josh!"

By June the Grays were at the top of the Negro National League standings. Gibson had a .391 average and had racked up a league high of seven home runs. But in the middle of the season, Gibson suddenly left the Grays to play baseball in Santo Domingo, capital of the Dominican Republic. He would be paid $2,200 for just seven weeks of work.

Gibson was not the only Negro league ballplayer to suddenly start playing in the Dominican Republic over the summer. A 1930 revolution had brought to power dictator Rafael Leónidas Trujillo. Trujillo had his own baseball team, but it was very weak. To try to look more powerful, Trujillo wanted his team to be the winners in the league.

Trujillo brought down Satchel Paige to play, offering him $15,000 for himself and another $15,000 to lure other Negro league players to the team. Unable to turn down the money, Gibson agreed to play with Los Dragones of Ciudad Trujillo. But unlike most players who jumped their contracts, Gibson asked the Grays' owner, Cum Posey, for permission, who reluctantly gave it.

Because the country was so politically unstable, Gibson and the rest of the team were kept under armed guard. They were barely allowed to leave their hotel and were guarded on the way to and from the ballpark. When antigovernment riots erupted during games in San Pedro de Macorís, Trujillo ordered the games stopped and ruled his team the winner by forfeit.

Despite the pressure, Gibson played well. Over the short season, he had an average of .453. But the other teams in the league were also strong. By the end of the season, the championship came down to a tough game against San Pedro. As Paige took the pitcher's mound, soldiers shot their rifles into the air. Paige said later he was terrified, wondering whether all the players would be assassinated if they lost the game. When the team fell behind 5–4 in the seventh inning, Paige recalled in his memoir, "You could see Trujillo lining up his army. They began to look like a firing squad." Luckily, Ciudad Trujillo managed to win the game 6–5.

In late July, Gibson returned to play for the Grays, who it seemed had no hard feelings. While he was out of the country, Posey had written a column in the *Courier* listing the players on his "all-time Grays team." Gibson made the list in three separate categories: catcher, right-hand hitter, and hardest hitter.

As was often the case, Gibson hit his stride late in the season. In August the Grays played against the Elite Giants in Fairmont, West Virginia. The *Afro-American* newspaper, covering the Grays' 8–4 win, reported, "Saturday's game featured Josh (Fence Buster) Gibson, who hit three home runs over [the] center-field fence in four times at bat." The three home runs came off pitcher Andy Porter, who was talented enough to play for eighteen seasons in the Negro leagues.

With Gibson's help, the Grays won the first National Negro League championship. Even with his seven-week stay in Santo Domingo, he had hit sixty-two home runs in the season. "The best we can do is to say Josh Gibson is the best baseball player, white or colored, that we have seen in all our years of following baseball," Posey wrote in the *Courier*.

The following year, Gibson did a long, question-and-answer interview with Posey for the *Courier*. But typical of Gibson, he supplied short, shop-talk answers and nothing else. Gibson revealed no personal or psychological information—no clues whatsoever about what made him such an awesome ballplayer.

Q. How does colored baseball at the present time compare with colored baseball at the time you broke in during 1930?

A. It is better now. We have a league now which we consider well organized. I feel as though I have something to play for now, besides just making a payday.

Q. What did you consider to be your best year?

A. 1931.

The hardest balls he had ever hit, Gibson told Posey, were at Yankee Stadium in 1930—he did not claim any went out of the park—and in a stadium in East Orange, New Jersey, in 1937. He also said he had played against so many major league players, there were "too many to remember."

When Gibson reported to San Antonio, Texas, in 1938 for spring training, he was put at third base for a short time to help strengthen the team's infield. But by May he was back to his usual position as catcher. In June the Grays were in first place in the league, and sportswriters were calling them one of the best teams in the history of black baseball.

Even as Gibson and the other Grays were performing amazingly well in the Negro league, the local major league team was falling short. The Pittsburgh Pirates came close to winning the National League pennant in 1937. How would the team have fared if Gibson and other African American players had been allowed to play on the team? By the mid-1930s, sportswriters were starting to ask that question.

Just before the 1938 season, Chester Washington of the *Courier* sent a telegram to Pittsburgh Pirate manager Pie Traynor. "Know your club needs players . . . Have answers to your prayers right here in Pittsburgh." Gibson was the first to be listed, followed by first baseman Buck Leonard and pitcher Ray Brown of the Homestead Grays and pitcher Satchel Paige and center fielder Cool Papa Bell of the Pittsburgh Crawfords. "All available at reasonable figures . . . would make Pirates formidable Pennant contenders." The telegram concluded, "What is your attitude? Wire answer."

But Traynor never bothered to reply. The Pirates finished the 1938 season in second place, two games behind the Chicago Cubs. Since then, baseball historians have enjoyed playing a parlor game about what might have happened if Pittsburgh had been smart enough to sign local black talent.

Compliments from white baseball professionals also rolled in steadily. In 1938, when the Grays played against a white team led by Brooklyn Dodgers shortstop Leo Durocher, Gibson hit three homers in the eight-game series. Durocher said afterward, "I played against Josh Gibson in Cincinnati, and I found out everything they said about him was true, and then some. He hit one of the longest balls I've ever seen . . . I'll bet you it's still sailing."

Leo Durocher played a major role in breaking baseball's color barrier. He was the manager for the Brooklyn Dodgers, the first major league team to have an African American player in 1947.

White sportswriters were also beginning to wonder in print why major league owners were being so stubborn about not signing black players, considering how much talent there was in the Negro leagues. In September 1938, Jimmy Powers, sports editor of the *New York Daily News*, famously wrote that Gibson would be worth $25,000 a year to any major league club.

A week later, Powers wrote another column in which he named seven African American ballplayers, including Gibson, who could step right into the New York Giants lineup and take the team to the pennant. In response, the *Courier* ran photos of all the players with the headline "Here's Jimmy Powers' 'Dream Team' for the New York Giants."

The possibility of the integration of the major leagues was complicated for owners of the all black teams. If the major leagues signed the best African American players, the Negro leagues would soon go out of business. One very influential black writer, Dan Burley of the Negro Associated Press, pointed out that most Negro league owners probably hoped that this would never happen, "and personally I don't blame them," he wrote.

Meanwhile, Gibson began to develop a drinking problem that was affecting his playing. In 1938 he won the most ballots among East players for the East-West game. But on the day of the game, Gibson was nowhere to be found. Posey announced that Gibson had come down with an unspecified last-minute injury. In fact he had drunk too much, overslept, and missed the train to Chicago. It was the first time that Gibson's drinking had affected his professional career.

Gibson hit another legendary home run in 1939. This was in a game against a semiprofessional team in Monessen,

Pennsylvania. The mayor of the town was in the stands. He had the game stopped so the distance of the hit could be measured. Depending on the version of the tale, the ball traveled either 512 or 575 feet.

JERRY GIBSON

Gibson's brother, Jerry, also had a brief career as a ballplayer. He was a pitcher for a semipro team, the Coraopolis Grays of Pittsburgh, in 1939. Later he pitched for the Cincinnati Tigers in the Negro American League.

Throughout 1939, sportswriters for African American papers kept up the pressure for the integration of the major leagues. When Negro leaguers with major league potential were mentioned by name, Gibson was always among them. An article in the *Courier* was typical. "If and when the major leagues open their doors to Negro ballplayers, there are two young men . . . who will, in all probability, lead the sepia parade into the big league fold. They are Josh Gibson and Buck Leonard of the Homestead Grays!" Later in the article, Gibson and Leonard were compared to Babe Ruth and Lou Gehrig of the famous New York Yankees of 1927.

Besides the constant comparisons to Ruth, Gibson was also occasionally compared to another major league player, catcher Bill Dickey of the New York Yankees. The sportswriter for the *Washington Post*, Shirley Povich, wrote that Gibson was the superior catcher. His opinion was seconded by Washington Senators pitcher Walter Johnson, who famously said that Gibson was worth $200,000. "He can do everything. He hits the ball a mile. And he catches so easy he might as well be in a rocking chair. Throws like a rifle. Bill Dickey isn't as good a catcher."

Not everyone agreed with Johnson's opinion on Gibson's catching. In an article titled "Gibson Is No Dickey," Sam Lacy wrote in the *Afro-American*, "A great hitter? Yes. A great catcher? No." As evidence, he cited a game in which Gibson missed three foul balls that should have been easy outs. "Josh is unquestionably a great hitter," Lacy wrote, "but for all-around play, he's no Dickey."

In August the second of two East-West games was played in Yankee Stadium. Jimmy Powers, sports editor of the *New York Daily News*, wrote about the upcoming game. The story, accompanied by a photo of Gibson, was printed in the Sunday edition of the nation's largest-circulation paper—another measure of how much attention white sportswriters were starting to pay to the Negro leagues. As a result of Powers's article, the East-West game was well attended by white baseball fans. About 20,000 fans were at the game.

When Josh Gibson Jr. was about ten years old, his father began to bring him to games and sometimes on road trips. But he was still not a doting father. "It was never like I played catch with him in the backyard or anything, he didn't have time for that," Josh Gibson Jr. recalled.

Powers's article added more layers of unreliability to the Gibson legend. The piece claimed that Gibson had hit eighty-four home runs in 1936—twenty-four more than Ruth's total—and sixty-three homers in 1939. "This man would be worth $25,000 a year to any club in baseball," he wrote.

Gibson's performance in the East-West game did not disappoint fans drawn by the Powers article. He hit two line drives that were caught, was walked intentionally twice, and finally hit a triple when the bases were loaded. All three runners made it home, helping the East to win, 10–2. Gibson ended the 1939 season with a .440 average, second in the league, and 16 home runs in league games.

When the season ended, Gibson went to Cuba to play with a team called the Negro National League Stars. In December he moved to Puerto Rico to play with the Santurce club. In the spring, the Grays expected him back, but instead Gibson decided to stay in Latin America.

A team from Caracas, Venezuela, had offered Gibson a contract for $700 a month, a $1,000 bonus, plus travel and living expenses. The offer was too generous to turn down. Again Gibson asked Posey for permission, who reluctantly gave it. Gibson hit .419 in the Venezuelan league, and though he was offered a three-year contract, he decided not to stay.

Posey thought Gibson would be back to the Grays by July, but instead he accepted an offer to play with the Mexican league for nearly $1,000 a month until November. Gibson remained in Latin America, completely missing the 1940 baseball season in the United States.

Meanwhile, even without Gibson, the Grays continued to be a strong team. Now known as the Washington-Homestead Grays, the team divided its home games between Forbes Field in Pittsburgh and Griffith Stadium in Washington, D.C. The Grays played in Griffith on Sundays when the Washington Senators were out of town.

Gibson returned home in January 1940 and signed a new Grays contract for $500 a month, which Posey announced was the largest salary ever given to an African American player. In the spring of 1941, the Grays headed to Orlando, Florida, to train, and Gibson was supposed to join them. But at the last minute, he got an offer from Club Azules de Veracruz, a team in Mexico City. Once again, although he had already signed a contract with the Grays, he signed another one with the Mexican team.

This time Posey lost his patience. He filed a lawsuit against Gibson seeking total damages of $10,000—the value of Gibson's house in Pittsburgh. In early May, the judge ruled against Gibson. He was ordered to return to the United States in six days to honor his contract, or he risked losing the house.

But Gibson did not return. He promised Posey he would be back for the 1942 season. He spent the summer season in Vera Cruz, Mexico. In the Mexican league, Gibson hit .374 and 33 homers in 94 games. After he led Veracruz to the championship, a Josh Gibson Appreciation Day was held in the city's Escambron Stadium. He was given the league's most valuable player (MVP) award, as well as the home run champion trophy.

When the season was over, Gibson played winter ball in Puerto Rico, where he had a tremendous streak, hitting a home run nearly every other game. There, too, Gibson was awarded

MVP and batting champion. No MVP awards were given out in the Negro leagues, and the honor meant a lot to him. Gibson saw his achievements in Puerto Rico as some of the high points of his career.

Chapter Eight

The Slide

In February of 1942, Gibson kept his promise and returned to play for the Grays. According to his contract, he would be paid $750 a month plus bonuses, which brought his earnings up to about $1,200 a month. The amount was even more than Satchel Paige was making and was almost in line with the major league salaries. The $10,000 damage suit that Posey had brought against him was quietly dropped.

According to his teammates, Gibson had first begun to have problems with his drinking while playing winter baseball in Latin American countries. Gibson had played winter ball every season since 1932. In Latin America, games were played only on Saturdays and Sundays, giving players a lot of free time during the week. And unlike in the United States, where teams had to spend hours at a time on the road, there was much less travel time between league cities. That meant Gibson had plenty of time to drink. Like his mother, Gibson seemed to have a drinking problem.

He also started experimenting with marijuana. Gibson was certainly not the only player to do these things. But in his case, the behavior seemed to be a sign of something serious.

Gibson began to demonstrate bizarre behavioral problems as well. According to one story, when he was in Puerto Rico, he went down to the main plaza and started taking off his clothes. When the police arrived, Gibson was so out of control he ripped the spare tire off the back of the police wagon. In another version of this story, when the police questioned the naked Gibson, he told them he was going to the airport. Rather than charging him with being a public nuisance, the league authorities suspended him from playing and sent him back to the United States.

By this time, the United States had entered World War II (1939–1945). African American ballplayers were beginning to return home from winter baseball. They either returned voluntarily or were ordered back by the draft board, which could draft men into the military. Gibson was not drafted, however. After twelve years of squatting behind the plate for hours a day, his knees were deeply scarred. He was declared class 4-F, which meant he was ineligible for any kind of military service.

When he returned from Puerto Rico, Gibson's physique clearly showed the signs of his heavy drinking. At 230 pounds, he even looked like the major league hitter Babe Ruth. But, just like Ruth, being out of shape did not affect Gibson's hitting. In his very first at-bat on returning to the Grays, Gibson hit a home run.

The discussion about integrating the major leagues continued to heat up. At the start of the 1942 season, Kenesaw Mountain Landis, the commissioner of major league baseball, announced that "there is no rule, formal or informal, no understanding, subterranean or otherwise, against hiring Negro players." Rumors abounded that the major leagues were on the verge of holding tryouts for African American players. Gibson, in his only known remark on the integration of the major leagues, told a reporter who asked him about the rumors, "I don't think they'd kid about a serious thing like that."

In July 1942, it seemed as if Gibson might actually get his chance. Gibson and Buck Leonard were called in to meet with Pittsburgh Pirates president William Benswanger. Benswanger had been quoted in the press saying that African American players were American citizens with the same rights as everyone else and that someone had to be the first to sign black players.

But nothing came of the meeting. Gibson never spoke publicly about what was discussed. Benswanger claimed afterward that Cum Posey had personally asked him not to sign Gibson and Leonard. With the best African American players gone to the majors, the Negro leagues would be decimated. This may have been the case, but to many in black baseball it just sounded like an excuse.

Around the same time, Gibson and Leonard had a similar conversation with Clark Griffith, the owner of the Washington Senators. The Senators at the time were very weak. Meanwhile, Griffith could look out his office window and see Gibson and Leonard hitting home runs again and again in his own field. In one game, Gibson hit three home runs at Griffith Stadium. One of them landed two feet from the top of the left-center-field bleachers, 485 feet from home plate. That season, he hit eleven home runs to left field—the deep field in Griffith Stadium—even though he only played there once or twice a week. According to some reports, this was more home runs than were hit to left field in all American League games in that park. Despite all of this, Griffith did not sign Gibson and Leonard to the Senators.

Sportwriters in the white press continued to call for integration, using Gibson as an example of what the majors were missing. Haskell Cohen, writing in a magazine called *Spot* in July 1942, pointed out that Gibson had hit home runs in all eleven major league ballparks where he had played. He was once again compared to Babe Ruth: "After twelve years in colored baseball, and at the age of thirty," Cohen wrote, "Gibson has compiled so many records with his hickory stick that it is doubtful if the great Babe himself did any better."

African American papers also kept up the pressure. In August, the *Courier* called Gibson "the No. 1 candidate for major league baseball." The paper even offered to pay Gibson's expenses to travel to any city where a major league team would give him a tryout.

❝Josh knew he was major league quality. We would go to a major league game if we had a day off. He was never the kind of a guy to say, 'I'm the great Josh Gibson,' but if he saw a player make a mistake he would say what should have been done, or he might say, 'I would have been expecting that.'**❞**

—TED PAGE, OUTFIELDER FOR THE CRAWFORDS

Meanwhile, according to Gibson's sister, Annie Gibson Mahaffey, Gibson and Hattie were married in Alabama during a Grays road trip in July of 1942. Mahaffey supplied this information to the Hall of Fame in the early 1970s. However, no documentation of the marriage exists, and other Gibson relatives, such as Josh Jr., didn't believe the event ever happened.

At the end of the 1942 season, Gibson's physical problems finally began to show in his playing. That year, the Negro World Series was held for the first time since 1927. The Monarchs, led by pitcher Satchel Paige, and the Grays squared off on September 8 at Griffith Stadium. In the run-up to the game, Gibson and Paige traded verbal barbs about who was going to best whom. But there was no contest at the game. Paige clearly came out on top. As Gibson walked up to the plate, Paige shouted at him that a fastball was coming. Gibson, convinced that Paige was trying to mix him up, prepared himself for a breaking ball. A few moments later, a fastball sped right past him: strike one. Soon after, Paige struck him out.

In his second at-bat, after two other players had managed to hit singles, Gibson was more successful. He hit one of his classic 420-foot blasts, but it was caught in the outfield. The Grays failed to score and lost the game 8–0.

At the end of the season, Gibson was clearly worn out. His knees were so damaged he sometimes had trouble getting into the proper catcher's crouch. Instead, he nearly stood up straight while waiting for the pitch. He was also suffering from headaches and fatigue. Gibson admitted that his drinking was affecting his hitting. But it didn't show in his statistics. At the end of the season, Gibson had racked up a .344 batting average, as well as a league high of 11 home runs. Nonetheless, he admitted to the *Afro-American* that he had noticed he had less control in the last season. "I just can't pull them to left this year," he said. "I'm hitting more balls to center than ever before. Gosh, I should hit some of them to right center, or even right field." For the first time since the start of his professional career, Gibson decided not to play winter ball. He needed time to recuperate.

If Gibson had hoped his health problems would improve after a winter off, he was unfortunately mistaken. On New Year's Day 1943, after an all-night drinking session, he had a seizure and lost consciousness. Gibson was taken to St. Francis Hospital in Pittsburgh where he lapsed into a coma. At first the doctors were not sure whether he was going to survive, but he regained consciousness later that evening.

According to his sister, Gibson was diagnosed with a brain tumor while at the hospital. They wanted to operate to remove it, but he refused, worried that he would end up paralyzed. After spending ten days in the hospital, he was released. He never spoke publicly about his condition. *The Pittsburgh Courier* reported that Gibson had suffered a nervous breakdown. According to the article, Gibson's health problems explained why he had failed to play his usual quality of baseball the year before—and even cost the Grays the Negro World Series.

As with so many other aspects of Gibson's biography, the real facts are unclear. His medical charts do not list a brain tumor among his ailments, only nervous exhaustion and hypertension. However, Gibson's doctor may not have included the information at Gibson's request. Or his sister, Annie, had the facts wrong, and he never had a brain tumor at all.

When the 1943 season began, Gibson's lethargy and headaches continued. But he still played hard. He always played in both games when the Grays were scheduled for doubleheaders, for example. His only concession to his health was that he sometimes played left field in the second game, rather than catcher.

In the middle of the season, Gibson hit another career high. He was featured in the July 19 issue of *Time* magazine. The only African American athletes to make it into *Time* before Gibson were Satchel Paige and the boxer Joe Louis. Many of the magazine's white readers learned for the first time that the Negro leagues had a player known as the black Babe Ruth. The article stopped short of calling for integration but pointed out that many white sports fans enjoyed the style of baseball played in the Negro leagues, including "their fancy windups, their swift and daring baserunning, their flashy one-handed catchups."

According to league figures, in 1943 Gibson hit .526 with 14 homers, which was a league high. But his unstable behavior returned. According to one story, Gibson hit a ball over the fence but ran around the bases the wrong way, starting with third base. He also repeated his old trick of walking around in public without clothing. Whenever his behavior got too out of control, Buck Leonard and a few other teammates would take him to St. Francis Hospital. His stays ranged from a day or two to up to two weeks. Amazingly, sometimes Gibson even played in the middle of these hospital stays. He came to the ballpark accompanied by attendants in white coats and then was sent back to the hospital afterward.

Despite his health problems, Gibson returned to playing winter ball in Puerto Rico in 1943. When he returned to the Grays for the 1944 season, he wouldn't play by the club's rules. He refused to go to spring training games. He claimed that after playing winter ball he did not need the extra practice.

Gibson's arrogance was difficult for the team's manager to take, but Gibson continued to perform well. That summer, he got one of his rare hits off Satchel Paige during a game in Chicago's Comiskey Park. The ball bounced off a large clock in the middle of the scoreboard—435 feet from home plate. As Gibson rounded the bases, he taunted Paige, "I love ya, man. If you could cook, I'd marry ya!"

By the end of his career, power hits had become so rare for Gibson that the unthinkable had happened—he had become a singles hitter. Unfortunately for Gibson, this happened around the same time that the Elias Sports Bureau began keeping accurate Negro league statistics. While his average was still an impressive .345, Gibson hit just 8 home runs, 5 triples, and 8 doubles in the 1944 season.

By 1945 Gibson was completely flouting training rules and had even brought his bad attitude to the games. When he was behind the plate, for example, he often did not even bother to chase pop flies, seemingly out of simple laziness. Other teammates had to cover for him.

But Gibson's hitting still remained solid. By the week of the July 29 East-West game, he was at .383, third in the league. But then Posey suspended Gibson just hours before the game was set to begin. According to W. Rollo Wilson, writing in the *Philadelphia Tribune*, Gibson had been suspended for a "steady infraction of training rules." The article even claimed that he had been asked to turn in his Grays uniform.

Satchel Paige had also been excluded from the East-West game. In previous years, an East-West game without the two biggest stars of the Negro leagues would have been unthinkable. But suddenly both Gibson and Paige were starting to seem like relics in black baseball. Both were beginning to be overshadowed by young, upstart players, such as the Kansas City Monarchs' twenty-six-year-old rookie shortstop, Jackie Robinson.

But Gibson had not been kicked out of the Grays. He ended the 1945 season with a .393 average, the best in the league. But the record also showed that Gibson had hit just four home runs in league competition that year.

The 1946 season was Gibson's last. Coincidentally, it was also the last season when the Negro leagues would seem relevant. The previous fall, Jackie Robinson had become the first African American player to sign a major league contract, with the Brooklyn Dodgers. Robinson spent the 1946 season playing with the Montreal Royals, a farm team for the Dodgers. A few of the owners of Negro league teams hoped that even after the major leagues were integrated, somehow the Negro leagues would be able to survive. But with the best players being picked off by the majors, most owners knew the end was near.

As if staging a last rally, Gibson hit some memorable home runs in 1946. In May, while playing against the Elite Giants at Baltimore's Bugle Field, Gibson hit a home run in the first inning. According to the *Afro-American*, it was "a smash that cleared the area roped off for the overflow crowd." Later in May, the *Philadelphia Tribune* reported a 440-foot hit against the Black Yankees in Griffith Stadium. The paper called it Gibson's second long homer in four days. He had hit a 457-foot home run in Forbes Field, also against the Black Yankees.

JACKIE ROBINSON

Jackie Robinson was the first African American baseball player in the modern-day major leagues. Born in 1919, Robinson went to college at the University of California in Los Angeles. He was the first athlete to win varsity letters in four different sports—baseball, basketball, football, and track. His career as a professional football player was cut short when he was drafted during World War II.

In 1945 Robinson began playing baseball with one of the top Negro league teams, the Kansas City Monarchs. Two years later, Robinson joined the Brooklyn Dodgers. Robinson was named Rookie of the Year in 1947 and the National League's Most Valuable Player in 1949.

Gibson ended the 1946 season with an impressive eighteen home runs, easily at the top of the Negro leagues. He played one final East-West game, in front of more than 45,000 spectators. In three at-bats, Gibson struck out three times. He ended his last season with a .361 average.

Exhausted, Gibson turned down an offer to play winter ball in Puerto Rico. He also passed on the chance to play with the Satchel Paige All-Stars against the Bob Feller All-Stars, one of the last black-versus-white competitions. With the integration of the major leagues, these race-based games were also on the way out.

OLDEST ROOKIE IN THE MAJOR LEAGUES

In 1948 Satchel Paige finally had the chance to play in the major leagues when he signed a contract with the Cleveland Indians. At age forty-two, his best years as an athlete were clearly behind him. But it meant a great deal for African American fans to see one of the greatest players of the Negro leagues finally have his moment in the sun. In the early 1950s, Paige pitched for the St. Louis Browns. In the late 1960s, he coached for the Atlanta Braves.

In December, Gibson turned thirty-five. His health problems had made him very weak, so he had to move back to his mother's house. In early January 1947, Gibson was ill again, this time with a combination of nervous exhaustion, kidney and liver dysfunction, and bronchitis. He had dropped down to 180 pounds. Toward the end of his life, Gibson began spending more time with his children, as if to make amends for the neglect of the previous years. He seemed to know the end was near, even as he tried to conceal his condition from his teammates and closest friends.

As with nearly every other aspect of Gibson's biography, there are multiple stories about how he died. Gibson's physician, Dr. Earl Simms, claimed that on January 19, 1947, he was summoned to a movie theater where Gibson had suffered a stroke. Gibson was then brought to his mother's house, where he never regained consciousness and died during the night.

Gibson's sister, Annie, told a much more dramatic story. In this version, Gibson came home and told his mother he was going to have a stroke. Gibson's mother told him not to be silly. Gibson went to bed to rest. Later, the family gathered at his bedside, talking and joking. Gibson wanted to see his baseball trophies again, which were scattered at the houses of various friends. So he sent his brother, Jerry, out to collect them. Then, with his family around him, Gibson's speech became garbled. He lay back and died at 1:30 A.M. According to the coroner, the cause of death was a brain hemorrhage, with hypertension as a contributing factor.

For three days after his death, Gibson lay in state at the Crunkleton Funeral Home, then for three more days in the home of his sister-in-law, Margaret Mason. A long line of friends, teammates, and fans filed through the house to pay their respects. The funeral service was held at the Macedonia Baptist Church—the same church where Josh and Helen Mason had married and where Helen's funeral had been held. According to another typical Gibson legend, his funeral was one of the largest ever in Pittsburgh.

Epilogue

Hall of Fame

In death, just as in life, Gibson became the subject of dramatic, unsubstantiated fable. This time the story originated with the sports editor of the *Courier*, Wendell Smith. On January 25, 1947, Smith wrote an emotional obituary of Gibson.

> Perhaps if Josh Gibson hadn't been a victim of the vicious color line in the majors; if he had been given the chance to make the big league he so justly deserved; if he could have swung his big bat against the type of competition for which he was born, he might be living today...I know the real reason Josh Gibson died. I don't need a doctor's report for confirmation, either. He was "murdered" by Big League Baseball!

Smith's interpretation of Gibson's death—that he had been a martyr in the era of segregated baseball—was adopted by

93

many Negro league fans and even by some of the players. But those who knew him well, including his close friends and his son, disagreed with that analysis. Gibson was just grateful to have the chance to play baseball, they claimed, and would not have brooded about the fact that he didn't get a chance in the major leagues.

On April 15, 1947, just three months after Gibson died, Jackie Robinson played his first game with the Brooklyn Dodgers. As predicted, the integration of major league baseball was the death knell for the Negro leagues. Slowly, the best African American ballplayers were signed to the majors. Some performed well, and others had mediocre careers. But black ballplayers were in the major leagues to stay. They no longer needed a separate league. Within two seasons, the Negro National League went out of business. The Negro American League survived until the mid-1950s but only as a shadow of its former self.

Meanwhile, Josh Gibson Jr. began to make a name for himself as a baseball player. In 1948, at eighteen years old, Gibson Jr. hit some tape-measure home runs just like his father, including a 425-foot hit. In the summer of 1948, he signed a contract to play second base for the Youngstown Colts, a farm team for the Cleveland Indians. Gibson Jr. became the first African American to play in the Mid-Atlantic League.

Unfortunately, Gibson Jr.'s promising career was cut short by injuries. Early in his rookie year, a pitch hit his head. He sustained a concussion and missed most of the rest of the season. After hitting .130 in eight games, hitting just 3 singles in 33 at-bats, Gibson Jr. was released from his contract.

He then played for a short time in the Negro leagues. In 1949 he was signed by the Homestead Grays. The Grays at the time was an independent team since its league, the Negro National League, had fallen apart. Gibson Jr. played for two seasons. He ended his short career playing for a farm team of the Pittsburgh Pirates in Farnham, Quebec. After he broke his foot sliding, he never really recovered his form and had to give up his dream of playing professional baseball.

By 1960 all of the major league teams were integrated. Ironically, integration also meant that Negro league baseball and Negro league stars like Josh Gibson were nearly forgotten.

Just a decade later, however, the golden age of black baseball was rediscovered. In 1970 the first definitive history of the Negro leagues was published, Robert Peterson's *Only the Ball Was White: A History of Legendary Black Players and All-Black Professional Teams*. Peterson dedicated an entire chapter of the book to Gibson, reviving the legend that he was responsible for the only fair ball hit out of Yankee Stadium. In the epilogue of the book, Peterson argued that "so long as the Hall of Fame is without a few of the great stars of Negro baseball, the notion that it represents the best in baseball is nonsense."

This oversight was corrected almost immediately. In 1971 Satchel Paige became the first Negro league player inducted into the National Baseball Hall of Fame. Although he had ended his career in the major leagues, Paige's most significant achievements had come as a pitcher on all-black teams. His induction renewed baseball fans' interest in an era of baseball that few knew about.

The following year, Gibson became the second Negro league player to be inducted into the Hall of Fame. His plaque reads:

Joshua (Josh) Gibson, Negro Leagues 1930–1946. Considered greatest slugger in Negro baseball leagues. Power-hitting catcher who hit almost 800 home runs in league and independent baseball during his 17-year career. Credited with having been Negro National League batting champion in 1936 –38 –42 –45.

Since then, Gibson's fame has continued to build. He is probably more famous now than he was when he was playing in the Negro leagues. Gibson's life and career have inspired several fictional films, including *The Bingo Long Traveling All-Stars and Motor Kings* (1976) and *The Soul of the Game* (1996). In 2000 the U.S. Postal Service issued a stamp that featured the images of Gibson and Satchel Paige.

While Gibson's exact statistics are in dispute, his contributions as an outstanding ballplayer are not. Gibson was more than one of the best players in the Negro leagues. He was one of the best players of all time.

PERSONAL STATISTICS

Name:

Joshua Gibson

Nickname:

Black Babe Ruth

Born:

December 21, 1911

Died:

January 20, 1947

Height:

6'1"

Weight:

210 lbs.

Batted:

Right

Threw:

Right

Position:

Center Field

BATTING STATISTICS

In 2006, the National Baseball Hall of Fame sponsored a study to try to reconstruct statistics for the Negro leagues. The following is the research team's best estimate of Gibson's batting statistics.

Year	Team	Games	At-bats	Hits	Home runs	Batting average
1930	Homestead	21	71	24	5	.338
1931	Homestead	32	124	38	6	.306
1932	Pittsburgh	49	191	62	8	.325
1933	Pittsburgh	38	138	54	8	.391
1934	Homestead	1	2	1	0	.500
1934	Pittsburgh	52	190	62	11	.326
1935	Pittsburgh	35	145	54	8	.372
1936	Pittsburgh	26	90	39	6	.433
1937	Homestead	25	97	41	13	.423
1938	Homestead	28	105	38	3	.362
1939	Homestead	21	74	27	10	.365
1940	Homestead	1	2	0	0	.000
1942	Homestead	42	138	42	7	.304
1943	Homestead	55	192	91	12	.474
1944	Homestead	34	123	44	9	.358
1945	Homestead	17	62	17	2	.274
1946	Homestead	33	111	32	7	.288

GLOSSARY

amateur: an athlete who plays without being paid

baseball statistics: data collected about each player's performance, including batting average, runs batted in (RBIs), and home runs

batting average: a measure of a batter's performance; the number of base hits divided by the number of official times at bat

cleanup hitter: the person who bats fourth in the batting order. This player is often one of the most powerful hitters on a team.

curve ball: a type of pitch that can curve either toward or away from the batter

doctored ball: a baseball that has been tampered with to make it harder to hit

doubleheader: a pair of games played back to back on the same day between the same teams

exhibition game: a game that is played for the fun of it and is not included in a team's ranking

fair ball: a ball that is hit between the first and third base lines

free agent: an athlete who can play with any team of his choosing

Jim Crow laws: laws that segregated white people and African Americans in the South

league: an association of teams that agrees to organize games for its members

mentor: an experienced person who gives advice

runs batted in (RBIs): the number of runners who scored on a hit

semiprofessional: an athlete who plays for pay on a part-time basis

stance: standing posture

strike zone: the area through which a baseball must pass to be called a strike (rather than a ball) if the batter misses it

SOURCES

2   Mark Ribowsky, *Josh Gibson: The Power and the Darkness* (Urbana and Chicago: University of Illinois Press, 2004), 41.

4   Ibid., 205.

6   Ibid., 23.

8   Robert Peterson, *Only the Ball Was White: A History of Legendary Black Players and All-Black Professional Teams* (New York: Oxford University Press, 1970), 161.

12   Ibid., 33.

13–14   Ibid., 39.

15   Ibid., 15.

16   Ibid., 160.

18   Ribowsky, 104.

23   Ibid., 29.

23–24   Ibid., 30.

24   Ibid., 32.

24–25   Ibid., 34.

25   Ibid., 33.

26   Ibid., 35.

34   Ibid., 45.

35   Ibid., 62.

35   Ibid., 60.

35–36   Ibid., 61.

36   Ibid., 64.

37   Ibid.

43   Ibid., 60.

44   William Brashler, *Josh Gibson: A Life in the Negro Leagues* (Chicago: Ivan R. Dee, 1978), 46.

44   Peterson, 158.

46   Brashler, 48.

46   Ibid.

49   Peterson, 164.

52   Ribowsky, 85.

52   Brashler, 61.

55   Ribowsky, 105.

57   Brashler, 73.

58   Ibid., 75.

60   Ribowsky, 135.

61   Ibid., 136.

61–62   Peterson, 160.

62   Ibid., 159.

65   Ribowsky, 167.

65   Ibid., 168.

67   Ibid., 177.

67   Ibid., 181.

67–68   Brashler, 111.

68   Ibid., 113.

68   Ibid., 114.

69   Ibid., 111.

70   Ribowsky, 185.

71   Ibid., 190.

71   Ibid., 191.

72   Ibid., 196

73   Brashler, 117.

73   Ribowsky, 200.

74   Ibid., 195.

74   Brashler, 119.

80   Ribowsky, 232.

80   Ibid., 234.

81–82   Ibid., 237.

82   Peterson, 168.

82   Ribowsky, 241.

84   Ibid., 247.

85   Time. "Josh the Basher," *Time*, July 19, 1943, http://www.time.com/time/magazine/article/0,9171,777882-1,00.html171,777882,00.html.,9171,777882,00.html (March 3, 2010).

86   Ribowsky, 267.

87   Ibid., 280.

89   Ibid., 288.

93   Ibid., 298.

96   Peterson, 254.

96   Ribowsky, 192.

BIBLIOGRAPHY

Brashler, William. *Josh Gibson: A Life in the Negro Leagues.*
    Chicago: Ivan R. Dee, 1978.

Peterson, Robert. *Only the Ball Was White: A History of*
    Legendary Black Players and All-Black Professional Teams.
    New York: Oxford University Press, 1970.

Ribowsky, Mark. *Josh Gibson: The Power and the Darkness.*
    Urbana: University of Illinois Press, 2004.

Riley, James A. *The Biographical Encyclopedia of the Negro*
    Baseball Leagues. New York: Carroll & Graf Publishers,
    1994.

WEBSITES

http://www.pace.edu/library/pages/links/ondisplay/josh.htm
This is an online version of a 2004 exhibit about Gibson from Pace University in New York.

http://espn.go.com/sportscentury/features/00016050.html
In this ESPN survey of top athletes of the last century, Gibson placed number 73.

http://www.nlbpa.com/gibson_josh.html
This site offers a brief biography of Gibson as part of the Negro League Baseball Players Association's site.

http://community.baseballhall.org/
All kinds of stats are available at the National Baseball Hall of Fame's website.

INDEX

Johnson, William "Judy,"
2, 18, 30, 31, 36, 52,
55, 65
Jones, Hattie (common-law
wife), 60, 82
Jones, Slim, 61

K
Kansas City Monarchs,
1–3, 28–29, 32, 47, 83,
88, 89

L
Landis, Kenesaw Mountain,
80
Leonard, Buck, 65, 69, 72,
80–81, 86
Lincoln Giants, 35–36
Louis, Joe, 85

M
Marshall, Jack, 45, 61–62
Mason, James, 26
Mason, Margaret, 26, 56
McGraw, John, 14
Mexican League, 75–76
Miami Clowns, 65
Montreal Royals, 88
Murdock Grays, 21

N
National Association of
Professional Base Ball
Players, 11
Negro American League, 94
Negro Leagues, 4, 11–20,
28, 38, 39, 52, 53,
67, 75
Negro National League, 14,
57, 75, 94
Negro World Series, 83
New York Amsterdam News,
6, 19
New York Black Yankees,
54, 55

O
Only the Ball Was White
(Peterson), 95–96

P
Page, Ted, 51, 61

Paige, LeRoy "Satchel," 46,
47, 55, 66, 69, 83, 85,
87, 90, 96
Peterson, Robert, 95–96
Philadelphia Stars, 47, 60,
64
Pittsburgh, 6–8
Pittsburgh Courier, The, 6,
19, 22, 67, 68
Pittsburgh Crawfords, 2, 22,
47, 50–64
Pittsburgh Pirates, 17, 21,
51, 69, 80
Porter, Andy, 67
Posey, Cumberland "Cum,"
2, 21, 32, 51–52, 64,
67, 68, 76, 80, 87
Powers, Jimmy, 70, 71
Puerto Rico, 56–57, 58, 75,
76–77, 78–79, 86

R
racism, 12–17
Rector, Cornelius "Connie,"
36
Robinson, Jackie, 88, 89, 94
Ruth, Babe, 36, 41, 42,
45, 72

S
Santurce Cangrejeros,
56–57
Satchel Paige All-Stars, 90
Smith, Wendell, 93
Sparrow, Roy, 3–4
St. Louis Browns, 47
Susce, George, 61

T
Tinker, Harold, 22–24, 41
Traynor, Pie, 69
Trujillo, Rafael Leónidas, 66
Turner, Wyatt, 24

W
Walker, Moses Fleetwood,
12
Walker, Weldy Wilberforce,
12
Washington, Chester, 69
Washington-Homestead
Grays, 75

Washington Senators, 81
Wells, Willie, 57
Williams, Smoky Joe, 2, 32
Wilson, W. Rollo, 35–36, 87
winter baseball, 56–57, 58,
75, 76–77, 78–79, 86
World War II, 79

Y
Yankee Stadium, 37, 61–62
Youngstown Colts, 94